P. P. Quimby

The *HEALING* *WISDOM*
of
Dr. P. P. QUIMBY

These ideas are in your mind
like little leaven.
They will work
till the whole mind is changed.

Second Edition

Edited by Mason Alonzo Clark

By selection of quotations from the Dresser and Collie
compilations of the Quimby manuscripts.

Frontal Lobe ®
Los Altos, California

First edition printing of 2000 in 1982
Second printing 2000 in 1984

Second edition – 2008

Library of Congress Control Number: 2008907606

ISBN: 978-0-931400-12-4

Printed in the United States of America

Mason Alonzo Clark
Frontal Lobe ®
Los Altos, California

TABLE OF CONTENTS

Note from the editor:

In this second edition the words of Dr. Quimby take precedence. Forewords and Editor's Notes have been placed in the rear along with history, bibliography, and concordance.

The words in this book are those of Doctor Park Quimby with obvious exceptions such as the "Searches" and the editor's notes well marked. Every effort has been made to keep sentences and paragraphs intact with their meanings unaltered while putting Quimby's notes into an orderly and readable form. It would be improper for this editor to modernize Quimby's English or to exclude passages that conflict with modern science and beliefs. The editor did see fit to set some of Quimby's words in a rough form of blank verse.

Many chapters are followed by quotations from great thinkers. The reader may compare their ideas with those of the New England healer. All were engaged in the Search for Truth.

The Introduction:

Doctor Quimby wrote several drafts of introductions for his intended book. One of these is printed as the introduction to the section titled Healing.

To open this book, I have collected from his own words what I believe might be the introduction Doctor Quimby would have written for this book. With obvious exceptions, all the words that follow are quotations from his notes.

*My object is to correct the false
ideas and strengthen the truth.*

God Made Everything Good

In introducing this work to the reader, my only excuse is the existence of evils that follow the opinions of the world in regard to man's health and happiness.

My object is to correct the false ideas and strengthen the truth.

I fitted out my barque some twenty years
ago and started without chart or compass,
Trusting to the wisdom of my experience,
determined to be guided by the inhabitants
of the land where I journeyed, and make way
to the passage that led to the other world.
Or to a new world on this globe.

Sometimes I was nearly exhausted
and on the point of returning,
When a light would spring up,
Or a solitary bird would sing
its beautiful notes from a clear sky,
While from this light came a mild breath
of pure air that would revive my soul.
In this warmth it seemed as though
I heard a voice say, "Come up hither."

My practice for twenty years has put me in possession of facts that have opened my eyes to the misery of mankind from ignorance of ourselves.

My object in introducing this work to the reader is to correct some of the errors that flesh is heir to. During a long experience in the treatment of disease, I have labored to find the cause of so much misery in the world.

In my investigation I found that my ignorance would produce phenomena in my subject that my wisdom would not correct. At first I found that my thoughts affected the subject, and not only my thought but my belief. I found that my thoughts were one thing and my belief another.

I ran against a stumbling block
  which upset all my theory
And left me without anything
  but the bare experiments.
I went to work to prove my belief,
And the experiments proved
  anything I believed,
And I concluded that man is just
  what he thinks he is to himself.

If I really believed in anything, the effect would follow whether I was thinking of it or not.

The reader will find my ideas strewn all through my writings, and sometimes it will seem that what I said had nothing to do with the subject upon which I was writing. This defect is caused by the great variety of subjects that called the pieces out; for they were written after sitting with patients who had been studying upon some subject, or who had been under some religious excitement, suffering from disappointment or worldly reverses, or had given much time to health from the point of view of the medical faculty and had reasoned themselves into a belief, so that their diseases were the effects of their reasoning.

I have patients with all classes of minds – with all types of disease. No two are alike. The articles are often written from the impressions made on me at the time I wrote.

To cure them was to show them the hypocrisy of their belief, and show that all men are to themselves just what they make themselves.

So my arguments are always aimed at some particular beliefs, sometimes words, sometimes one thing, again another. Hence what I write is like a court-record or a book on law with the arguments of each case. I take up a little of everything.

I have said many things in regard to medical science but all that I have said was called out by my patients being deceived by the profession. The same is true of the religious profession. My writings are not to establish any religious creed or bolster up any belief of man. They are simply the outpouring of a truth.

The science of curing the disease has never been described by language, but the error that makes disease is in the mouth of any child. In fact, the theory of correcting disease is the introduction of life.

Within the last seven years I have sat with more than twelve-thousand different persons and have taken their feelings and know what they believe their diseases were and how each person was affected, but I knew the causes.

It is not a very easy thing to forsake every established opinion and become a persecuted man for this Truth's sake, for the benefit of the poor and sick, when you have to listen to all their long stories without getting discouraged. This cannot be done in a day. I have been twenty years training myself to this one thing, the relief of the sick.

A constant drain on a person's feelings for the sick alters him, and he becomes identified with the suffering of his patients: this is the work of time. Every person must become affected one way or the other, either to become selfish and mean, so his selfish acts will destroy his wisdom, or his wisdom will become more powerful.

It is not an easy thing to steer the ship of wisdom between the shores of poverty and the rocks of selfishness. If he is all self, the sick lose that sympathy which they need at his hand. If he is all sympathy, he ruins his health and becomes a poor outcast on a charitable world. For the sick can't help him and the rich won't.

Here you see the true character of Wisdom. It shrinks not from investigation, although it is unpopular and has the whole world to contend with.

If it were in my power to give to the world the benefit of twenty years' hard study in one short or long letter, it would have been before the people long before this. The people ask they know not what. You might as well ask a man to tell you how to talk Greek without studying it.

You may ask, if all I say is true what is it good for? If it is only a belief, I admit that it is of no more value to a person than any religious belief. You may ask for proof that will give some light upon the subject.

I will give it, as near as a man who has eyesight can explain color to a blind person.

*I make war with what comes in contact
    with wealth and happiness,
Believing that God made everything good.
And if there is anything wrong
    it is the effect of ourselves.*

*Man is responsible for his acts
    and even his thoughts,
Therefore it is necessary
    that man should know himself
    so that he shall not communicate sin or error.*

*This is my theory:
    to put man in possession of a Science
That will destroy the ideas of the sick
    and teach man one living progression
    of his own identity,
With life free from error and disease.*

Part 1 – Principles

Awake from your lethargy.
Come to the light of Wisdom.

Chapter 1

What is Happiness?

Everyone must answer

What is happiness? It is what follows any act of the law of science, but it is not always understood. As a person's happiness is the effect of his knowledge, to be good is the fruit of Science.

Happiness is contentment, not life or death.
Misery is discord, not Wisdom but error,
If then you attach your life to an error,
  like distributing life to the body,
Then your life is unhappy
  according to the loss.
If our happiness is from wisdom
  it becomes a part of ourselves,
But if it is from a belief,
  it is adopted and we may lose it.

We often hear people say that their religion makes them happy. But if religion is anything outside of ourselves it contains neither happiness nor misery. Can any person define what he gets except that it is a belief? A belief that will make one person happy will make another miserable.

Look at any religious society and you will find that the individuals cannot agree in belief. So those who cannot agree are slaves to those whose authority they admit as their rulers.

The cause of man's misery and trouble lies in our false reasoning. It always has and it always will be so till man is convinced that his happiness depends on Wisdom, and his misery on belief.

People never seem to have thought that they are responsible for their belief. To analyze their beliefs is to know themselves, which is the greatest study of man. All theories for the happiness of man contain more misery than happiness, either directly or indirectly.

To destroy the beliefs of man is to leave him where God left him: to work out happiness by his own wisdom.

Our opinions are the foundation of our misery, while our happiness is in the knowledge that follows solving the problem of error. To illustrate, when solving a problem you have an opinion, and are in trouble about it. But when the answer comes the happiness accompanies it. Then there is no more death, or ignorance, sorrow, or excitement. Error and ignorance have passed away, all has become new, and we are as though we never had been. We have all the happiness we want; the misery is gone, and the spirit returns to the Great Spirit, ready to solve another problem.

Happiness is dependent on externals, but lies within us, and is the consciousness of keeping our loftier impulses free from contamination, and revealing in our acts a strength which arises from uncorrupted motives.

Every one must answer
for his own sins or belief.

Our beliefs are the cause of our misery.
Our happiness and misery
are what follow our belief.

If I can show that man's happiness is in his belief and his misery is the effect of his belief, then I shall have done what never has been done before. Establish this and man rises to a higher state of wisdom not of this world, but of that world of Science which sees that all human misery can be corrected by this principle, as well as the evil effects of error. Then the Science of Life will take place with other sciences.

Instead of your happiness being in the world, the world's happiness is in you. Here is your true position, and this is the struggle you will have to go through. Shall the world lead you, or shall you lead the world? This is the point that is to be settled in your mind.

Many shall come in the name of the Truth, and say, do this, or do that – music, dancing, and all sorts of amusements. But the truth says beware, be not deceived, seek first the truth, and all the above will be a pleasure to you.

This is a trying scene to go through; it seems as though you must leave all the world's pleasure, and seclude your self from society. But this is not the case; you will like society all the better.

This will make you love amusement for the sake of doing good. Then you will rejoice with those that rejoice and weep with those that weep, and your happiness will be their happiness. Then you will be loved and respected for your love or knowledge, then you will draw around you those minds that are in harmony with yours.

What is your source of happiness? The twentieth-century mathematician and philosopher Bertrand Russell ends his book the *Conquest of Happiness* with this conclusion:

The happy man is the man whose personality is neither divided against itself nor pitted against the world. Such a man feels himself a citizen of the universe, enjoying freely the spectacle that it offers and the joys that it affords, untroubled by the thought of death because he feels himself not really separate from those who will come after him.

It is in such profound instinctive union with the stream of life that the greatest joy is found.

Happiness may have different sources for different people, but one concept is repeated in the writings of philosophers, seers, and Doctor Quimby. A modern seer, L. R. Hubbard wrote:

Happiness is the overcoming of not unknowable obstacles toward a known goal.

The philosopher Arthur Schopenhauer made a similar observation:

To overcome difficulties is to experience the full delight of existence.

Chapter 2

If Science Rules

Life and happiness is the reward

A man may be scientific in many sciences, mathematics, chemistry, astronomy – all that are acknowledged and admitted by even the natural man, though not understood. But the Science of Happiness is not acknowledged by the wisdom of the five senses. It requires more senses to put men in possession of this Science that will teach him happiness. As happiness is what follows a belief, it is necessary to know whether our wisdom is of this world of opinion or of the world of Science.

This world sees nothing outside of its senses. Wisdom sees nothing of the natural man's senses but ignorance, so that the wisdom of this world is opposed to the Science of Happiness.

I wish to make you understand
  these two characters: Science and opinion.
See which you follow: for you must follow one.
You cannot serve both at the same time.
If you serve Science,
  you are in your wisdom and know it.
If you serve opinion, you have no wisdom,
  but your life is in a belief
  that can be destroyed.

The two worlds may be divided in this way:
One opinions – the other Science.

Opinions are matter or the shadow of Science.
One is limited in its sphere,
And the other knows no limits.

The one is today, and tomorrow is not.
The other is an endless progression.

The one is always changing,
The other is always progressing.

If we know the true meaning of every word or thought we should know what will follow. So a person cannot scientifically act amiss. But being misled by public opinion, we believe a lie and suffer.

How do I know I have got hold of a true method? How do I know I am not mistaken?

There are many reasons which confirm my method as a science. One is that I constantly improve it. I find I can cure more quickly, and harder cases.

To teach Science is to put it in practice so that the world shall be put in possession of a truth that shall be acknowledged above the natural man.

By establishing the law of science we destroy the law of ignorance. To introduce a Science that explains the errors that keep us in trouble is what the prophets foretold, and wise men have looked for ever since the world began.

By the gospel of Truth, Science will have all saved – not from the Christian world – but from this world of superstition and ignorance, saved for the greater truth that was prepared from the beginning of the world for all those who search and try to find it.

You cannot go into the clouds to call it down, nor into the sea to call it up, but it is in you, in your very thoughts. It is not of this world, but of a higher state, that can penetrate this earthly matter as light through darkness.

In mathematics, chemistry and all the arts and sciences that can be demonstrated, knowledge submits to wisdom, but that part of man's senses attached to knowledge that is not subject to science is in ascendancy in religion, disease, and politics. These are false sciences based on opinions. They are the same that Jesus denounced as false prophets, evil and blind guides who deceived the people.

Astronomy has destroyed some of the hideous features of religion and introduced a happier state of society, but it was not the design of astronomy to destroy religion.

Still it is the natural result of science to destroy error and prejudice.

Now it is not to be expected that every person who happens to think of flying can make a flying machine that will be successful. Nor is it certain that any invention to control the elements will always work so that accidents as they are called will not take place and lives lost and much trouble made before Science is established. Ideas come forth and the minds are affected, and try for the prize.

Science, like an under-current,
is deep and strong.
And as its tide advances, it will
sweep away the foundations of aristocracy.
Revolutions must come,
And no man can tell what will be the end
of this generation.
But Science will work out the problem
of universal freedom to the oppressed
in body and mind.

All Science is spiritual and is not known by the priests and demagogues or doctors. The theories of these three classes are not based on wisdom but on opinions.

Now Jesus cured the sick and said if they understood Him they might do the same. We want a theory like that of Jesus not of talk but of works, for a theory that cannot be put into practice is worthless.

In the 1921 and 1961 editions of The Quimby Manuscripts, edited by Horatio W. Dresser, what is printed is "not of talk but of <u>words</u>." The editor was certain this was an error in transcription because Quimby could not have meant "words." Dr. Seale kindly provided a photocopy of the original handwriting of Quimby which plainly shows "works." See the Bible quotation on page 80 regarding the word-work controversy.

Every science has its standard, based on actual knowledge, not on opinion. They prove their wisdom by their works.

Science cannot admit what cannot be proved.

Error is a wilderness filled with all kinds of superstition. Science is the axe in the hands of Wisdom to hew down the wilderness and destroy its inhabitants and introduce a better state of society.

The world of opinions is the old world. That of Science is the new, and a separation must take place and a battle fought between them. The world of error and opinions has held Science in bondage ever since man began to be independent of savage life.

Ideas come forth and the minds are affected, and try for the prize. For instance the idea of navigating the air. All minds are excited. Experiments are tried; accidents, as they are called, happen and lives are lost to this world of error.

But that which governs life cannot be lost, but must mingle in with the idea of progression – not losing its identity. What man loses in weight or matter, he makes up in science or knowledge.

All Science is a part of God.

If Science rules,
   life and happiness are the reward.

Science is Wisdom put into practice.

The most famous scientist and a famous priest of the twentieth century have these comments about science:

The scientific method can teach us nothing else beyond how facts are related to, and conditioned by, each other. The aspiration toward such objective knowledge belongs to the highest of which man is capable. Yet it is equally clear that knowledge of what is does not open the door directly to what should be.

Religion, on the other hand, deals only with evaluations of human thought and action; it cannot justifiably speak of facts and relationships between facts. Science without religion is lame. Religion without science is blind.

— Albert Einstein

One might well become impatient or lose heart at the sight of so many minds remaining today still closed to the idea of evolution. Blind indeed are those who do not see the sweep of a movement whose orbit infinitely transcends the natural sciences. Evolution is a light illuminating all facts, a curve that all lines must follow.

I do not propose today to deal directly with the question of discovering what it is that makes science valuable, and even indispensable, for the full development of the Christian; all I shall try to do is to make you love science in a Christian way.

— Father Teilhard de Chardin

Chapter 3

The Light of Wisdom

The principle that never moves

The two characters: wisdom and opinion, stand before each other, and the people choose the one they will obey, just as they do in national affairs.

Awake from your lethargy.
Come to the light of Wisdom.

Man's happiness is in himself.
Life is eternal, Life is Wisdom.

Wisdom is progression.
Its enemy is ignorance.

Seek Wisdom.
Believe no man's opinion.

As God is Wisdom,
Wisdom is Science.

Our beliefs, thoughts and opinions can change. So when we say a person never changes, it is as much as to say he is only a brute.

Then what is it that does not change? It is the Principle that never moves. It is that which says, when we have found out something new: "Why did you not find it out before?" It says to us when we are investigating certain mathematical truths: "This truth has always existed," and we believe it. This something is Wisdom.

Wisdom is the true man and error the counterfeit. When Wisdom governs matter, all goes well. When error directs, all goes wrong.

Here is the conflict: whether man's opinion is to rule, or his wisdom. How many persons are there in this city who get up in the morning and pass the day without gaining enough wisdom to last them till nine o'clock? No man should have any credit over his fellow men unless he shows some superiority over the errors of his age.

The man who is rich in this world's goods to the exclusion of some scientific capital cannot travel in the world of Science with his money.

Wisdom contains no opinion or selfishness. Like charity, Wisdom has no ill will towards its neighbor, but – like the rays of the sun – is always ready to impart heat to all who will come to the light.

The Wisdom that acts upon the mind is something that never has been described by a language, but is looked upon as a superior "power." This power gives rise to all religious opinions. Man has tried to condense it into a being called "God," and he worships it.

Opinions are like a shadow.
The true substance is God.

True wisdom is attached to the substance,
False wisdom to the shadow.

This world is the shadow
of Wisdom's amusements.

Two-thousand, three-hundred and seventy years ago, in Book Seven of his Republic, Plato gave us the allegory of the cave:

In the cave were a captive people whose only knowledge of the world was their understanding of shadows they saw on the wall of their cave. These shadows came from a puppet show that mocked reality. In their ignorance they supposed these shadows and the echoes of their sounds to be the truth.

One of the captives was dragged out of the cave into the sunshine. He was at first blinded by the light, then slowly learned the truths of the real world. He returned to the cave to tell his friends.

Upon first re-entering the cave, he was blinded by the darkness. Seeing his confusion, then hearing his assertions about the falsity of the shadows, the cave dwellers laughed at him and scorned him. They determined never to go from the cave and to kill anyone who tried to lead them out.

Plato probably had in mind the killing of Socrates.

All great thinkers and observers have encountered cave dwellers. Doctor Quimby's healing work dealt with their problem: false beliefs. These false beliefs – shadows, not Wisdom – he found to be the cause of disease and all problems.

In a later chapter Quimby tells of his experience with the opposition of the "cave dwellers" of his day.

Chapter 4

God

The essence

The Wisdom of God does not go into the clouds to call truth down, nor into the deep to call God up, but shows us that *God is in us, even in our speech.*

To give the truth I must make the reader detach his senses from a God of man's belief and attach them to this invisible Wisdom which fills all space, and whose attributes are all light, all wisdom, all goodness and love, which is free from all selfishness and hypocrisy, which makes or breaks no laws, but lets man work out his own salvation; which has no laws and restrictions and sanctions men's acts according to their belief, and holds them responsible for their belief, right or wrong, without respect to persons.

To know that God cannot be divided is to know that we cannot be separated from our Heavenly Father. To know God is to know ourselves and to know ourselves is to know the difference between Science and error. Error is of man and truth is of God.

God is truth and there is no other truth.

He is all Wisdom and nothing else.
All other things having form
  are things of His creation.
His life is attached to all
  that we call life.

Now where is the God
  in whose Wisdom I believe?
He is in the hearts of the people.
He is not a man, neither has He form.
He is neither male nor female.
God is a Spirit and not a man.

My God speaks in this way. He has finished His work or machine and sits down to see it work.

It needs no repairs. It will run and perform its work till every one shall know that to be good is to be wise and man's color is not the problem of progression but wisdom. And wisdom when reduced to practice will be recognized by every wise and benevolent person without regard to color.

God is not a man
  any more than man is a principle.
My God is Wisdom
  and all Wisdom is of God.
Where there is no wisdom there is no God.

God is the name of a man's belief and our senses are attached to our opinions about our belief or God. The God of the savages is their belief; the God of the Mohammedans is their belief, and so too the Christian's God.

Man has invented a God
 according to his belief
So that God is the embodiment
 of man's belief.
As man's belief changes
 so his God changes,
But the true God never changes.

The Christian's God, like themselves, is like a house divided against itself. The God of the North and the God of the South are as much at war as the Christian's worshipers; each prays to God for help and each condemns the other. Thus it is plain that gods of this kind are a farce and all our worship of such is from a superstitious fear of a tyrant whose name we dare not take in vain.

I will give you the religious or political God. He is represented as watching the movements of the armies and dictating to the heads of nations. No one approaches him except the ordained priest.

The time will come when the true God will be worshipped in spirit and truth, for God is a spirit and not a man.

Man's God is all the time
 listening to his prayers
 and setting all sorts of trouble.
My God does not act at all.

He has finished His work and leaves man to work out his happiness according to his own wisdom. God or Wisdom has never made anything to torment mankind. Error has created its own misery.

Where is one to find knowledge of God? A great American essayist and retired minister, Ralph Waldo Emerson advised the seniors of the Harvard Divinity School:

Once leave your own knowledge of God, your own sentiment, and take secondary knowledge as Saint Paul's or George Fox's or Swedenborg's, and you get wide from God with every year this secondary form lasts.
Let me admonish you, first of all, to go alone.

The Roman emperor Marcus Aurelius wrote his knowledge of God while leading his troops against tribes on the northern border of the empire:

All parts of the universe are interwoven with one another, and the bond is sacred. Nothing is unconnected with some other thing. For all things have been coordinated and combined to form the same universe. There is one universe made up of everything, and one God who pervades everything, and one substance, one law, one common reason in all intelligent animals, and one truth.

Called "the greatest modern philosopher," Benedict de Spinoza had an excellent education in theology and philosophy but earned his living as a grinder of lenses. Park Quimby, also a mechanic and worker in science, probably never read Spinoza and may never have heard of him. In Spinoza's *Ethics* we find his understanding of God:

(continued)

(continued)

By "God" I mean a being absolutely infinite. Besides God, no substance can be granted or conceived. Whatever is, is in God, and without God nothing can be. God is the indwelling and not the transient cause of all things. Things have been brought into being by God in the highest perfection, inasmuch as they have necessarily followed from a most perfect nature.

God's nature and existence, and consequently His providence, cannot be known from miracles, but they can all be much better perceived from the fixed and immutable order of nature.

An exiled Jesuit Father of the twentieth century, Father Teilhard de Chardin became a paleontologist and geologist, and wrote this while scientific advisor to the Geological Survey of China:

The doctors of the Church explain that the Lord deliberately hides himself from us in order to test our love. One would have to irretrievably committed to mental gymnastics, one would have never to have met in one's own self or in others the agonies of doubt not to feel the hatefulness of this solution.

No: God, I am quite certain, does not hide himself so that we shall have to look for him – any more than he allows us to suffer in order to increase our merit.

Chapter 5

Mind

The medium of a higher power

I found that by the power of my own mind I could change the mind of my patient and produce a chemical change in the body, like dissolving a tumor.

Now the word *mind* is not the substance, only the name of the substance that can be changed. The world makes mind intelligence, that is, direction. I put no intelligence in it, but make it *subject to intelligence.*

Mind is a spiritual matter which, being agitated, disturbs the spirit. The mind, being the matter under the control of the spirit, is capable of producing any phenomena.

The word *fire*, for instance, doesn't mean the substance to be consumed but the process of consuming it. So mind is the name of a spiritual substance that can be changed.

The idea that matter and mind make the man prevents man from understanding himself. The time has nearly arrived when the people will be prepared to receive a great truth that will give an impulse and set them investigating a subject which will open to their minds new and enlarged ideas of themselves and show man what he is and how he makes himself what he is.

All persons are to themselves just what they make themselves.

The body may be compared to a dead weight,
The mind to a lever.
It is error to put knowledge into the lever.
The mind is a medium of a higher power.

Our bodies are the machines to be moved,
Like a locomotive, our mind is the steam.
The steam contains no knowledge.

A higher power governs the mind and body,
As the engineer governs the steam and the engine.

The mind is the medium of a higher power independent of the natural man that is not recognized. When we speak of mind, we embrace this power, as we often do in speaking of the lever, supposing the power to lie in the lever, not thinking that the lever contains no knowledge or power.

We are all taught to believe that mind is wisdom and here is the trouble, for if mind is wisdom then wisdom cannot be relied on, for all will admit that the mind changes.

Mind to me is not wisdom,
  but spiritual matter.
It is this: all opinion, belief, reason,
  everything that can be changed.
Mind, like the earth,
  is under the direction of a higher power,
Which is subject to Wisdom.
The world calls it God.

A Case: "a needle extracted"

What proof is there that man's wisdom and senses are not in the body but outside of it and in the mind? I will relate a fact which will prove it.

I once put a lady to sleep that she might have a needle extracted from her arm. During the operation she said to me: "Does it hurt you?" The person who spoke was the one who was looking on, for she could describe all that was transpiring. If it should be said that it was myself who spoke through her, I will admit that she expressed my very thoughts, but if I could speak through her body, why could not she speak through mine? If so, the body of each was only the shadow of our belief and – I thinking it might hurt her and she thinking it hurt me – we were therefore neither of us hurt from the fact of sympathy.

Philosophers, theologians, and scientists have struggled to understand the nature of the human mind. Is the mind something separate from the body? What is the relation of the mind to God? Who controls the mind? No better explanation is to be found than that of Doctor Quimby. The great philosopher, Benedict de Spinoza, warns us not to be too soon troubled by new ideas:

The human mind is part of the infinite intellect of God, thus when we say that the human mind perceives this or that, we make the assertion that God has this or that idea, not in so far as he is infinite, but in so far as he is displayed through the nature of the human mind.

Note: Here I doubt not, readers will come to a stand, and will call to mind many things which will cause them to hesitate; I therefore beg them to accompany me slowly step by step, and not pronounce on my statements, till they have read to the end.

Bertrand Russell, a twentieth-century philosopher, warned us that:

Not only will men of science have to grapple with the sciences that deal with man, but – and this is a far more difficult matter – they will have to persuade the world to listen to what they have discovered. If they cannot succeed in this difficult enterprise, man will destroy himself by his half-way cleverness.

Chapter 6

What We Believe

The greatest study

What we believe, that we create.

Beliefs make us act,
   and our acts are directed by our beliefs.

> *Man is governed by two powers*
>   *or directions, One by a belief,*
> *The other by a science.*
>
> *A belief contains no wisdom*
> *But is a shadow of something*
>   *that cannot be seen,*
> *Worshipped by man*
>   *who knows not what it is.*
>
> *There is a vast difference*
>   *between a belief and knowledge.*
> *Knowledge is wisdom*
>   *and contains no belief.*
> *A belief is error.*
> *The only way to detect them*
>   *is by their works or fruits.*

Make man responsible for his beliefs and he will be as cautious what he believes as he is in what he sees or does.

Whatever is true to a person, if he cannot prove it, is not necessarily true to another. Therefore, because a person says a thing is no reason that he says true.

When you have arrived at a truth, if you find it attached to a belief, you may know it is not a truth, for it may change.

But this is a truth: A belief may be changed.

The magicians and sorcerers cured by their belief. They thought their power came from a spirit-world. They believed that disease was sent into the world to torment mankind.

The priests had the same belief. They held up to the people the idea that they must do something different from living honestly and dealing with mankind as though we were one family, that a certain belief was necessary to keep us clear of hell, which itself had been invented to torment man.

This doctrine kept the people in ignorance of themselves and made them nervous, giving rise to belief in evil spirits.

God or Wisdom has never made anything to torment mankind.

I believed as all others did, but my theory and practice were at variance with each other. I therefore abandoned all my former beliefs, as they came in contact with my practice, and at last followed the dictates of the impressions made on me by my patients. The unraveling of my old opinions gave me knowledge of myself, and happiness the world knew nothing of, and this knowledge I found could be taught to others. It teaches man that he is not in the body, but outside of it.

People never seem to have thought that they are responsible for their beliefs. Make man responsible for his belief and he will be as cautious what he believes as he is in what he sees or does. To analyze their beliefs is to know themselves, which is the greatest study of man.

If man knew himself his first object would be to become acquainted with sensations that affect him. He would then learn that a corrupt fountain cannot bring forth pure water, and that from aristocracy nothing but the blackest corruption can issue, which however is becoming popular because of the fountain.

To separate us from the error, and bring us into harmony is to explain the false idea away, and then all sorrow will pass away, nothing will remain save the recollection of what is past like a dream or nightmare, and you will not be likely to get into the same error again.

If you embrace the world
  you embrace its errors,
And become a servant to its laws,
The spirit or truth departs
  to the God that gave it.

But if you hold on to the Truth
  the world is in subjection to you.
And instead of becoming a servant,
  you become a teacher of Truth to the world,
To lead other minds to the Truth.

A Case: "a sharp, stinging pain"

If two persons agree upon anything, they call it a truth, but the truth is in them and not in the discord or thing believed. For instance, two persons believe that there is such a thing as a ghost. Now if they believe it, it is the truth to them, but it is not certain that the ghosts exist outside of themselves. The word "truth" used in this way applies to all sorts of error, but there is another mode of testing the word scientifically. I will give a case where the right and wrong truth come in, for the word is only to assent to what one or more believe. I will show how I tell the word.

A patient calls on me. I sit down by her and I feel a sharp stinging pain in my breast. This I tell to the patient as her feelings. This she says is true. So here is a real truth without a belief for its basis.

I now tell the patient that she thinks the pain arises from a cancer coming in the breast. The patient says "yes." Now here is another combined truth for it combines the two—the fact that she believes she has a cancer and that I know she does.

But in this there is a discord for I know there is no truth in it, but the truth is in her belief. So the discord is in these two truths. It is also a truth to me that there is no cancer. Now to destroy the belief of a cancer is what I try to do. My reason is to destroy one truth that is founded on a belief and establish health and then she will enjoy it.

See page 107, "Doctor P. P. Quimby and His World," describing the state of the science of medicine in 1865. Dr. P. P. Quimby would welcome modern medicine.

The problem of beliefs that Doctor Quimby observed in his patients has been recognized by modern savants as diverse as the Indian, J. Krishnamurti, and the American third-force psychotherapist, Carl Rogers. Krishnamurti tell us:

Belief is one thing and "what is" is another. Belief is a word, a thought, and this is not the thing, any more than your name is actually you. Your belief in God will give you the experience of what you call God.

You will always experience what you believe and nothing else.

Belief comes from fear and is the most destructive thing. Belief divides people, makes them hard, makes them hate each other and cultivate war. A mind clouded by fear of belief is incapable of any kind of understanding, any realization of what truth is.

When the mind is free of belief then it can look.

Carl Rogers, like Park Quimby, experienced the enlightenment of changed belief:

My belief has developed and altered, until now it is almost the antithesis of what I was taught – and believed – in my youth.

Charles Darwin quoted Marcus Aurelius (a Roman Emperor) on the effect of thought:

Such are thy habitual thoughts, such also will be the character of thy mind; for the soul is dyed by the thoughts.

Part II – Healing

*The minds of individuals
mingle like atmospheres.*

Young P. P. Quimby mesmerizing his favorite subject, Lucius Burkmar. This experience gave him the knowledge that led to his career as a healer and teacher. He found he could heal without mesmerism and without an assistant. He tells us: *"I found that any medicine would cure if he (Lucius) ordered it. This led me to investigate the matter and arrive at the stand I now take: that the cure is not in the medicine, but in the confidence of the doctor or medium."* This discovery was the beginning of Quimby's work as a healer.

Chapter 7

Introduction Regarding Healing

by Doctor Quimby

In order to understand Dr. Quimby*, it is necessary to give the reader some idea in regard to how he treats diseases and also some explanation as to the way in which he says they were brought about. To do this, I must give his ideas of the cause of disease. This will enable the reader to see some meaning in his otherwise blind writings for he reasons about things that would seem to many persons as having nothing to do with the cure of disease.

His ideas are entirely new to the world and if no explanation or introduction to his writings is made, the reader would, of course, pass over what he says with indifference and condemn it as visionary. It is, therefore, necessary to set the reader right at the outset, lest he should weary in looking for the principle the doctor claims to have discovered.

Dr. Quimby asserts and expects to prove that what is called disease is not a cause but an effect. He says that thoughts are like the shock of a galvanic battery, that they

---

* Here, and in some other instances, Dr. Quimby writes of himself in the third person. This Introduction is quoted verbatim from the Collie transcription, page nine.

are directed by some wisdom outside of the individual and that these thoughts are deposited according to the direction, and bring about a phenomenon. This phenomenon which he calls an "idea" is named "disease".

He says that every idea, whether of disease or of anything else is a combination of thoughts, and that every person is responsible to himself for his ideas and must suffer the penalty of them.

Dr. Quimby's theory is to correct those ideas which are false and avert the evil that flows from them. He holds that disease is caused by false ideas over which we have no control and that a different mode of reasoning from that which now prevails will eradicate from society the phenomena called disease.

In treating the sick, Dr. Quimby introduces the subjects of religion, politics, and all ideas, the discussion of which agitates society. These, he says, contain fear and excite the mind which, by a false direction, brings about the phenomenon called disease. Thus it is evident his ideas are at variance with the belief of the world, so he stands alone, his hand against everyone's and all against his.

He takes every patient as he finds him and commences as a teacher with a pupil destroying his error by correcting every idea that affects his health. He often comes in contact with pet ideas of the patients, like religion for instance, that is so interwoven with the patient's existence that they have become a part of him. If these cause the patient trouble, it is the doctor's business to correct them.

Chemical changes he talks a great deal about. This phrase he makes use of gives the patient an idea of the change in the system which always accompanies a change of ideas. He says that every idea or belief affects people just in proportion to their capacity to understand. He also says that obstinacy often prevents people from taking an interest in what they hear, thus protecting them from disease.

The doctor shows how fear also affects the mind. He says that false ideas contain some bugbear of which people are afraid and this he has to battle with; and in order to destroy this bugbear which terrifies them, he is obliged to destroy the idea which contains it.

Patients, he says, will cling to their ideas as a child to its mother and he sometimes has sharp discussions before they will yield the point. This discussion he calls the remedy so he says that the curing of disease is a scientific mode of reasoning. His theory is to correct man's errors so far as health and happiness is concerned.

His first principle is that nothing cannot produce something. Life, he says, is not a reality but an idea and in it is the fear of destruction called "death". He claims that life and death are no part of wisdom for the words cannot apply to what never had a beginning or ending. . . .

August 1864

Chapter 8

The Creating of Disease

The invention of man

Every disease is the invention of man
and has no identity in Wisdom,
But to those believe it
it is the truth.

All disease is only the effect of our belief. Disease is an error the only remedy for which is the truth. Disease is the natural result of ignorance and error governed by discords of the mind.

The belief is of man and as Science sees through man's belief it destroys the belief and sets the soul or wisdom free.

Diseases are like fashions, and people are as apt to take a new disease as they are to fall in with any new fashion.

All persons believe in disease and their belief is in the thing believed. All diseases have an identity and the well are likely to be deceived. But these diseases are in the mind as much as ghosts, witchcraft, or evil spirits, and the fruits of this belief are seen in almost every person.

I know that a belief in any disease will create a chemical change in the mind, and that a person will create a phenomenon corresponding to the symptoms. Conventional cures have been by the same remedy. Disease being brought about through a false belief, it took another false belief to correct the first; so that instead of destroying the evil, the remedy created more.

I will stop here and say a word or two about a young man that first called to see me. I sat down and found him very much frightened and nervous from a little sensation and suffocation. He thought he had heart disease and when I told him what it was and all it amounted to, he was all right.

Now if it was not for this evil in the mind, there would not have been cause of alarm and if I had not explained, he might have died at almost any time for he said it would wake him up two or three times in the night.

Now I say that science calls these evils lies and the sick have been made to believe that the very things or evils that they bring on themselves by their own acts are something that has come upon them without any of their action when it in reality is that they are the author of their own existence.

You tell me I "look sick."
You tell me that people often die
  with just such a feeling as I have.

By mesmerizing me into your belief,
  you disturb my mind
And create the very idea you have invented.

. . . At last I die – just as you foretold. . . .
All this is disease. And you made it.
If I had never seen you,
* I should not have died.*

Take the small-pox. The first sensation upon the patient contains neither opinion, happiness nor misery. The cause was one of the natural results of motion which might be traced back through many changes containing no more harm than any breeze that reaches man at any hour, but it gives a start to the mind like the fall of weight.

According to the world there is such a disease as small-pox. With God or Wisdom this must be truth or it must be a lie, or belief in a lie. No one will believe that Wisdom can have small-pox.

Small-pox is like a tree whose fruits are scattered abroad infecting those who eat them. It is a superstitious idea and like all such it has a religious cast. It deceived the world that all might be saved or vaccinated. As many as received the virus or were baptized with the belief were saved. Here is introduced another world which is deliverance from small-pox. To all who passed from their old belief into the world of vaccination there is no fear of death from small-pox, but a fear lest they have not been vaccinated with genuine virus. Now what does their salvation rest upon? It rests on no principle outside the mind. In ignorance of causes, people are satisfied with someone's belief that there is virtue in this savior. Thus their minds are quiet and the fruits are a milder disease.

Small-pox is a reality to all mankind. But I do not include myself, because I stand outside where I can see things real to the world and real with Wisdom.

I tell you a lie which you believe and an effect follows; this does not prove that I told the truth because the effect is seen. For instance, I tell you that you have small-pox. This shocks you and you are really frightened. A phenomenon attends or follows the fright. The physicians are consulted and they pronounce the disease small-pox. To you and to the world this is proof that it is small-pox. But to me it is only proof that you believed a lie.

In 1981, it was announced by the World Health Organization that small-pox had been eradicated by means of vaccination. No cases were to be found anywhere on the face of the earth and none should ever occur again. Humankind had been freed from the disease that had mutilated and killed millions.

Doctor Quimby would change his belief, as he admonishes us to do.

There is a vast difference
between a belief and knowledge.
Knowledge is wisdom
and contains no belief.
A belief is error.
The only way to detect them
is by their works or fruits

But this is a truth: A belief may be changed.

I have been 20 years in the practice of curing disease and learning the cures and I have learned that nine-tenths of the sick at this time would be well and hearty if the medical faculty were annihilated.

Neuralgia is one of the commonest diseases of the day, but this is giving way to a new invention called the spine disease and there have been such improvements that this has lost its identity in the new inventions of human diseases. This has opened a field for the medical faculty. There cannot be a female of any respectability but she must be insulted by these quacks with the idea that she has this disease in some form or other.

... falling of the womb, internal ulcers, ovarian tumors, weak spine, heart disease, etc. Now I say, and stand ready to prove, that all the above diseases are made up by the medical faculty for their special benefit. A more miserable humbug was never invented and men and women pay their money to these quacks for what never had an existence outside the profession. These diseases were never known to the people 70 years ago but now every female is liable to be affected by these diseases.

The medical faculty has been the means of lowering the female character for they feel guilty and ashamed of themselves for they have been made to believe a lie and they can't help it.

Man is made up of truth and belief. If he is deceived into a belief that he has or is liable to have a disease, the belief is catching and the effect follows.

My theory teaches man to manufacture health. When people go into this occupation, disease will diminish. Those who furnish disease will be few and scarce.

The creating of disease is under the superstition of man's belief.

I have said that fear produced a chemical change in man's belief and as a matter is one element of his belief, this is liable to take form according to the belief.

It has always been impressed on children that ghosts are seen in the burying grounds. This belief makes an atmosphere over the dead like a cloud on a mountain and in a certain state of mind, certain persons can make a ghost as easily as a certain state of the atmosphere will make the boreals, which always keep just as far from the traveler.

So it is with spirits, when you get where they are. They are gone but the atmosphere still remains and persons may feel it.

A Case: "afraid of these devils"

I once visited a sick man, it was about eight o'clock in the evening when I visited his room. Immediately upon entering, the atmosphere of the room produced such an effect on me that I felt as though my hair stood on end, and it seemed as though the room was full of spirits. As I approached the bed, he seemed frightened.

"You are frightened to death," I said. "Why do you lie here?" He said he couldn't get up.

I said, "You are afraid of these devils. They scare you and when I came in they left and are now standing out among the apple trees."

"They scare you a little," he said. This was a fact. He then said, "These devils have taken me by the nape of my neck and seat of my pants and laid me here, but I never told of it before."

I told him to get up and I would keep them away. He did so and got well.

In 1864, Pasteur proved the existence of infectious microbes. But, near the end of his life, Pasteur remarked:

The microbe matters less than the mental and physical ground in which it is let loose.

A distinguished British surgeon of the twentieth century, Sir Heneage Ogilvie has commented:

A happy man never gets cancer.

In 1860, the most eminent professor of medicine was Dr. Oliver Wendell Holmes at the Harvard University Medical School. He had these hard words for the tools of his trade:

I firmly believe that if the whole materia medica, as now used, could be sunk to the bottom of the sea it would be all the better for mankind – and all the worse for the fishes.

Chapter 9

Children Are Not Exempt

Persons affect each other

The child is an idea of the father and mother, it is a child of circumstances and liable to all the evils of its parents. Cure the world of these evils called disease and you introduce a generation of children composed of elements as much superior to the generation of these times as man is superior to the brute.

Children are not exempts, they suffer if they are in the vicinity of the disease, for their parent's sins. Their diseases are the effect of the community. These results come from the older inhabitants who embody the superstitions of the world, and they are as tenacious of their beliefs.

There is a language that has never been reduced to words. For instance, the feelings of a sick child cannot be described, yet every one is confident that the child feels sick. A doctor is called and the little child is treated according to his ideas which are explained to the mother. If she believes the physician, she begins to torment the child by her own mind or belief which she received from the doctor. So a new disease is formed that is for the benefit of anyone except the child.

The trouble is the result of language. To cure the child is to take the feelings and to explain them to the mother, showing her how she has been deceived. Then she ceases from doing evil and learns to do right.

It is an undisputed fact which philosophy has never explained, that persons affect each other when neither are conscious of it. According to the principle by which I cure the sick, such instances can be accounted for, and it can be proved beyond a doubt that man is perfectly ignorant of the influences that act upon him, and being ignorant of the cause is constantly liable to the effect. To illustrate this I will relate a case that came under observation.

A Case: "its parents' belief"

A woman brought her little son, about five years old, to be treated by me. When I sat with the child I found his symptoms were similar to those which people have in spinal or rheumatic troubles. But the child being ignorant of names, and having no fear of disease could only describe his feelings in this way: he complained of being tired. Sometimes he said his leg was sore and sometimes his head was tired. To me his feelings were as intelligent as any odor with which I am familiar.

I described his feelings to his mother, telling how he would appear at times. This she said was correct, and feeling impressed with the truth I told her, she said she would sit with me and see if I were equally correct in describing her case. I found that the mother had precisely the same feelings as the child, yet she complained of disease which the child never thought of, and furthermore she had not the least idea the child had such feelings.

To prove that I was right about the child, I told her to ask him if he did not feel so and so when he would lay his head down, and she found I was correct. These were the mother's symptoms: a heavy feeling over the eyes, a numbness in the hands, weakness in the back, and a pain going from the foot to the hip, all accompanied by a feeling of general prostration. To her every sensation was the effect of a sort of disease, yet every sensation she had, the child had also, but he had not attached names to them.

After playing, his leg would pain him, and he would be restless at night; while his mother reasoned from the same feelings that she had spinal disease, trouble of the heart, and was liable to have paralysis. If she had been ignorant as the child of names, she would have been well; for all its trouble came from its mother, and her trouble was from the invention of the medical faculty.

It may be asked, how could the child be affected by its mother? In the same way I was affected. To have the sense of smell or any other sense, requires no language. An odor can be perceived by a child as well as by a grown person.

* * * * * * *

The wisdom of the world acts in this way: it puts its own construction on all sensations produced in the mind, and establishes its knowledge after the effect is produced.

For instance, a child feels a pain in its head, the child has no idea what it is, and if the mother is as ignorant of its origin as the child, no effect of any moment is produced. But the wisdom of the world arrives in the form of a lady.

She hears the account of the pain from the mother, and assuming a wise look gives her opinion in regard to the trouble, and says the child is threatened with dropsy of the brain, because she shows the same symptoms of another child who died of that disease.

This account excites the mother, whose mind acts upon the child. The explanation of the wise lady gives direction to the mind, and presently the work commences to show that she is right. A doctor is called who is as wise as the lady, and not being willing to be outdone by her, he puts in a few extras like congestion of the brain, says the lady was right but did not get the whole of the matter. So he has two chances after the child is killed to prove his superior wisdom over the lady.

I contend that the child has no dropsy of the brain, but only some slight shock upon its mind, and quieting the child is all that is necessary for a cure. Here the controversy ends. If the mother employs me, I prove my theory and the child gets well. If they prove theirs, they kill the child and an examination is made which establishes their theory, and I am a humbug or quack. If I take the case, and the child gets well, "the child was not sick, only a little nervous."

The child is affected by its parents' belief, which is as real an enemy to health as slavery is to freedom.

A Case: "I must cure the mother"

To show the effect of the will upon the mind of a child, I will state the case of one about two years old who was brought to me to be treated for lameness. The mother held the child in her lap and informed me that it was lame in its knee. This was the information I received from its mother; but when I sat by the child I experienced a queer feeling in the hip and groin, but no bad feelings in the knee. I told the mother that the lameness was in the hip, and that I would show her how the child walked, and how it would walk were it lame in the knee. I then imitated the walk of the child, and also showed how it would walk were the lameness in the knee. After I explained the difference to her the mother admitted I was right.

I then informed her that to cure the child's lameness I must cure her (the mother) of the disease which was in her senses while the phenomenon was exhibited in the child. She said the doctor told her the disease was in the knee, and ordered it splintered. To splinter up the knee and keep it from bending would be to encourage the evil in the hip, and make a cripple of the child. I was obliged to explain away the doctor's opinion. When I succeeded in doing that, it changed the mother's mind so much that when she put the child down she could see that her will guided its motion. This was so apparent to her that she could, in some measure, counteract the wrong motion of the child. With my wisdom attached to the child's will I soon changed the mind so that the child walked much better.

Sir William Osler, perhaps the most eminent medical practitioner of the twentieth century, commented on the art of healing:

The psychical method has always played an important, though largely unrecognized, part in therapeutics. It is from faith, which buoys up the spirits, sets the blood flowing more freely and the nerves playing their part without disturbance, that a large part of all cure arises. Despondency, or lack of faith, will often sink the stoutest constitution almost to death's door; faith will enable a spoonful of water or a bread pill to do almost miracles of healing when the best medicines have been given over in despair. The basis of the entire profession of medicine is faith in the doctor, his drugs, and his methods.

Plato attributes to Socrates and a physician of Thrace the advice:

You ought not to attempt to cure the body without the soul for the part can never be well unless the whole is well. All good and evil, whether in the body or in the human nature, originates in the soul, therefore you must begin by curing the soul. This is the great error of our day, that physicians separate the soul from the body.

Two-hundred years earlier, Solon, the Greek statesman, land-reformer, and poet wrote:

The smallest hurts sometimes increase and rage
more than all art of physic can assuage;
Sometimes the fury of the worst disease
the hand by gentle stroking will appease.

Chapter 10

Sitting by a Patient

My cures are in my belief

There is a principle or inward man that governs the outward man or body. When these are at variance or out of tune, disease is the effect, while by harmonizing them, health of the body is the result. This can be brought about by sympathy and all persons who are sick are in need of this sympathy.

To the well these remarks will not apply, for the well need no physician. By these remarks I mean a well person does not know the feelings of the sick, but the sick alone are their own judges. And to every feeling is attached a peculiar state of mind which is peculiar to it. These states of mind are the person's spiritual identity, and this I claim to see and feel myself.

Doctor Quimby, with his clairvoyant faculty gets knowledge in regard to the phenomena which does not come through his natural senses, and by explaining it to the patient, gives direction to the mind. And the explanation is the science or cure.

When sitting by a patient I feel the sensation in my mind, and immediately a figure or spirit is made which is reflected as an impression on my body. Now if I were not aware of the cause I might think I was the author or orig.-nator of this horrid belief. But knowing that it is only the reflection from my patient's mind, the idea dies.

Doctor Quimby never accuses any one of imagining that they are sick. He admits every sensation that a person may claim. Indeed he takes their feelings himself, so he has positive proof that they exist independently of what the patient says.

My theory teaches me to look upon you as an intelligent creature. I take upon myself all your feelings and see all your troubles. By my theory or truth I come in contact with your enemy and restore you to your health and happiness. This I do partly mentally and partly by talking till I correct the wrong impressions and establish the Truth, and the Truth is the cure. I destroy the disease by showing the error and showing how the error affects the patient.

My cures are in my belief or wisdom. And the patient's disease is in his belief or knowledge.

I will state a case. A man uses tobacco freely, both chews and smokes. His wife, being of a sympathetic nature enters into his error to try to reform him. This brings her into the same company that he is in. This is taking a disease from sympathy and it shows that such evils are catching in the world.

To such I stand in this way. I take the symptoms and know who is the devil. I expose him, the devil leaves, and the patient is cured. Show a man who smokes or chews just how habit affects him and he will part company with tobacco. I feel that if you were aware of the evil influence of the enemy that is prowling around you, enticing you to smoke, you would not harbor him one moment, but hurl him from you as you would a viper that would sting you to the heart.

I know that opinions are something and they are our friends or our enemies. So the opinion you have of smoking is a false one and is an enemy to you. It is like the serpent that coils around you like a boa constrictor till you feel its grasp around your chest, making your heart palpitate and sending the heat to your head. Then you will struggle to rid yourself of his grasp.

Then there are other classes of diseases that cannot be cured so easily. Rheumatism that affects the legs so much that the joints become stiff – such I would advise to stay at home if they think to be cured at one or two visits. All bedridden persons that have the use of their limbs but cannot walk from weakness I have cured very soon, but those that are paralyzed on one side or both had better stay at home for the expense will be more than the good they will be liable to get. Persons smoking or chewing, if they have any disease that they would have me treat, independent of tobacco, I can cure but if they are well and choose to smoke or drink or chew, it is none of my business. It is a matter of their own, but if they are sick, then if I find that tobacco hurts them, I almost always cure them at the first sitting. If any person is nearly gone with consumption, I should advise him to stay at home unless it is to be relieved of the distress.

There are a great number of sick who are not able to be cured; for man's life and happiness in this enlightened world (made so by the medical profession) made dollars and cents the test, so if a man has not these he must suffer.

I have observed the effect of medicine
and have found that there is more virtue or misery
in the advertisement than in the medicine.

If physicians would investigate mind
a little more and medicine a little less,
they would be of some service.

The cure is not in the medicine,
but in the confidence of the doctor.
All medicines affect the body only
through the mind.
All drugs when taken stupefy the intellect,
so that science cannot reign.

When Miller prophesied the end of the world, ninety-nine of a hundred were affected to some extent. This was shown by the count taken by the churches. Even the Unitarian Universalists had their meetings and men and women spoke who never spoke before and probably never will again. But it showed what man's belief can do.

Dr. Q. comes to the sick as a pilot to the captain of a ship in a storm or fog, when dangers thicken and inevitable destruction threatens. He learns the trouble from the captain, and quieting the crew by his composure, inspires them with confidence, gives them directions, and brings them into harbor.

Lest there be doubt, these two paragraphs are copied verbatim from the transcriptions, Collie p.249 (May 1862) and Dresser p.192 (Jan 1860). As elsewhere, this book is in Quimby's own words.

A Case: "by religious excitement"

I often find patients whose disease or trouble was brought on by religious excitement. I went to see a young lady during the Miller* excitement. She was confined to her bed, would not converse with any person, lay in a sort of trance with her eyes rolled up in her head, took no notice of any person; the only thing she would say was that she was confined in a pit, held there by a large man whose duty it was to hold her there, and she said to me, "I shall never die, nor will never get well."

She had been in this condition for one year, refused all nourishment, and was a mere skeleton at the time I went to see her. This was her story when I got her so as to converse. I sat down by the lady, and in about an hour I saw the man she had created, and described him to her, and told her that I should drive him away. This seemed to frighten her, for she was afraid for my safety. But when I assured her that I could drive the man away, she kept quiet. In three hours she walked to the door, and she recovered her health.

---

* In 1831, William Miller began to prophesy the end of the world. It was a popular idea in the first half of that century. He finally set the date for March 21, 1844 and that was a night of panic for thousands of his followers. Doctor Quimby saw many patients affected by the "Miller excitement" – fearful or disappointed. From that excitement came the Seventh-Day Adventists, now proven to be enjoying better than average health and freedom from diseases. From them we are learning. God acts in most marvelous ways.

Chapter 11

A Clairvoyant State

The minds of individuals mingle

Every phenomenon in the natural world has its birth in the spiritual world.

The greater number of influences which act upon us do not come through the natural senses, and are all the more dangerous because unknown.

The basis of Dr. Quimby's theory is:

That there is no intelligence, no power or
  action in matter of itself,
That the spiritual world to which our eyes
  are closed by ignorance or unbelief
  is the real world,
That in it lie all the causes for every
  effect visible in the natural world, and
That if this spiritual life
  can be revealed to us,
In other words if we can understand ourselves,
  we shall then have our happiness or misery
  in our own hands;
And of course much of the suffering
  of the world will be done away with.

Every man has two selves, one acknowledged by the natural man, the other by the spiritual man.

A clairvoyant state is different from the natural state. Persons in a clairvoyant state can talk; they have every faculty which they possess in the waking state. Space and time may or may not be annihilated.

If man could retain his reason and natural senses, and at the same time be conscious of the other state, he would be a man beside himself, thus making two living intelligences in one identity acting through one. Thus the clairvoyant man could correct the errors of the man of flesh and blood and keep him in subjection to his wisdom.

To make a good clairvoyant one must,
*   beginning on earth,*
Rid himself of all beliefs and
*   every theory of man,*
And as he sees the absurdity of his own opinions
He becomes lighted up
*   in another atmosphere on a higher plane*
Where he feels the discords of this world.

He then becomes sensitive to the errors
*   and opinions of man,*
They affect him, and his spiritual senses
*   act independently of his natural will or senses,*
Then he is two persons.

This is my state as far as regards the sick. When I sit by the sick and take a patient by the hand, I feel a sensation. This affects me and the sensation is produced by something coming within my senses as a man of flesh and blood. This excites the spiritual or scientific man, and the senses, being freed from matter or opinions, see the natural man or opinion that causes the trouble.

As I retain two identities, I see the error and explain it to the natural senses. These are set at rest and harmony is restored.

I cannot find language to explain this so that you will understand it. I will now take a rose for an illustration.

You are like a rose. You throw from yourself
an atmosphere or vapor.
As the rose throws off its peculiarities to
the air, the world judges of its odor.
So as man throws off his peculiar character
of life: health or disease,
The world is to judge of his happiness or
misery by the fruits of his belief.

The minds of individuals mingle like atmospheres.
And every person's identity exists in this atmosphere.

Spiritual matter surrounds every person and contains an expression of character. What we perceive without the aid of the natural senses is the mind or spiritual matter, or atmosphere, or vapor, or whatever you choose to call it, that surrounds everyone and is an index of character. This is what we come in contact with in our intercourse with men, and through this medium we influence others and are influenced ourselves. It contains opinions, thoughts, and everything in us which can be changed.

Can Dr. Quimby be in two places at the same time? My answer is "I can" by sitting by the sick, not the well, for a sick person is one beside himself and to converse with two persons who are not aware of their presence, one must be in communication with both.

I have two identities, one in matter and the other out of matter, one can be seen and felt by the natural man and the other can feel and see the sick man's identity, which to him is not visible to his natural man.

What is a clairvoyant person?

It is being conscious of his own existence
as a living, thinking, seeing, intelligent creature.
And this is not seen by the natural man.

Then what is the natural man?

He is the shadow of the clairvoyant,
neither are conscious of the existence
of both at the same time.

Why do you speak of two when one is only a shadow?

The clairvoyant is like a man who is
just where he thinks he is;
The natural man is governed by a belief.
Reason does not enter into the
combination of the clairvoyant

Where is my consciousness?

I am conscious of my senses in both states
at the same time, and change the former.
I do not see my own shadow,
but I see myself as I really am to myself
and knowing that I am not as I ought to be,
I change that knowledge by comparing
myself to health till I feel it.

Health is the standard by which we judge ourselves and accordingly as a man deviates from this standard, he is in the dark and makes shadows. These shadows are the feelings of the sick man called "disease."

It is an undisputed fact which philosophy has never explained, that persons affect each other when neither are conscious of it.

According to the principle by which I cure the sick, such instances can be accounted for. It can be proved beyond a doubt that man is perfectly ignorant of the influences that act upon him, and being ignorant of the cause is constantly liable to the effect.

By thoughts we are all affected, and even by the settled opinions of people, whether they trouble themselves to apply them to our case or not.

Now when I sit down by a diseased person,
I see the spiritual form, in this cloud,
*   like a person driven out of his house.*
They sometimes appear very much frightened,
*   which is almost always the case*
*   with insane persons.*
I show no disposition to disturb them
*   and at last they approach me cautiously,*
If I can govern my own spirit or mind,
*   I can govern theirs.*
At last I commence a conversation with them.
They tell me their trouble and offer
*   to carry me spiritually to the place*
*   where their trouble commenced.*

A Case: "the scene of her troubles"

I was sitting by a lady whom I had never seen until she called upon me with her father to see if I could help her. The lady had all the appearance of dropsy. I took her by the hand. In a short time it seemed as though we were going off some distance. At last I saw water. It seemed as though we were on the ocean. At length I saw a brig in a gale. I also a man on the bowsprit, dressed in an oil- cloth suit. At last he fell overboard. The vessel hove to and in a short time the man sank.

This was a reality, but it happened five years before. Now to cure the lady was to bring her from the scene of her troubles. This I did and the lady recovered.

With the arrival in Paris in 1778 of Viennese physician Franz Anton Mesmer, the history of psychotherapy began. Mesmer introduced the modern world to the power of suggestion and exposed the unconscious mind to examination.

As Mesmer was crossing from the magical world of astrology, through the excitement of the new electricity and magnetism, to the science of the mind, he wrote:

Man possesses properties analogous to those of the magnet. He is endowed with a sensitivity by which he can be in contact with beings who surround him, even those who are farthest away. The principle of this action, considered as an agent acting on the inmost substance of nerves of the animal body, could become a means of curing, and even of defending oneself from sickness.

Carl Rogers, after finding his way from the dogma of the psychotherapy guild to a greater truth, tells us:

I find that when I am closest to my inner self, when I am somehow in touch with the unknown in me, when perhaps I am in a slightly altered state of consciousness, then whatever I do seems to be full of healing. Then, simply my presence is releasing and helpful to the other . . . it seems that my inner spirit has reached out and touched the inner spirit of the other. Profound growth and healing and energy are present.

Chapter 12

The Opposition of All Opinions

The great obstacle

What has a man to contend with
  who undertakes to establish a new science?
He has the opposition of all opinions
  of the world in regard to it,
  and all their influence.

He will be misunderstood by fools,
  and misrepresented by knaves,
For his science will tear down their
  fortress of belief.
And they will use all their skill
  and deception to defeat their enemy.
Their weapon is their tongue,
And the tongue of a hypocrite is, of all weapons,
  the most deadly to truth;
For it can assume the form of an angel
While it is sapping your very life's blood
  from your soul.
Its life and happiness are its own torment.

Ever since the world began,
  science has had this enemy to contend with,
And some very hard battles have been fought
  before error would leave the field.
Even when forced to retreat into darkness
  it would come out.

To fight the life of error like a soldier and contend for the truth of Science requires more courage than it does to fight for your own bread.

Science first comes to the educated, but they have no light to distinguish between truth and error and cannot receive it. So it turns to that class which has no prejudices and here in the wilderness it develops itself until it has attained its growth and then comes forth.

Then commences the war between the educated, who are ignorant of the truth, and Science. While Science is growing in the minds of the people, its opponents are eating and drinking, gloating over their spoils, till the tide of popular opinion sweeps away their foundation. They never seem to realize their house falls over their heads.

The medical faculty reason: "Do not destroy the medical constitution, for you will let in a swarm of quacks that will get the world in a horrid state. The regular physician will have no standing and sickness and death will triumph over the land."

The ministers also exclaim: "Do not touch the Divine institution, for religion is all that keeps the world from going to destruction."

Wisdom replies: "I will laugh at your fears, and I will pour out light like wrath and cut you off from the face of the earth and give the earth (or mind) to a more enlightened people, who will obey the laws of Science and teach others to do the same."

The world will oppose this Science.
It will be crucified by the church,
Hated by doctors,
Despised by the proud,
Laughed at by fools,
And received by the foolish of this world.

The blind guides, who have eyes but cannot see, ears but cannot hear, and hearts but cannot understand Science are afraid of the truth lest it destroy them, for the death of error is the introduction of the Science of Life and Happiness.

The great obstacle in establishing a new science in the understanding of the people arises from their ignorance. Science always has had to contend with this difficulty. To the scientific mind a superstition about anything that science has explained is nothing. But to the unscientific mind it may be truth. But if Wisdom casts out error, true Science will stand.

I have said that, when any new idea comes up, a class of persons enter into the investigation of it but very few are ever able to put the idea into practice or get the prize, though most all can understand something of the theory. There is a vast difference between talking a theory and talking *about* a theory. Talking about a theory is like talking about a science we do not understand; it contains no wisdom.

The medical faculty, spiritualists, and every class who have wit enough to have a belief, keep up a warfare to keep their beliefs alive that they may obtain a living.

Physicians will admit what the people believe. They will acknowledge I cure, but limit my power to a few nervous cases, and appeal to the vanity of intelligence by saying that it is not possible that an uneducated person can really cure actual disease.

Religious sects fight for their various beliefs which contained not a word of truth and the world has to suffer the consequences.

So in the church the religion of Jesus' Science is never heard; for it would drive aristocracy out of the pulpit, and scatter seeds of freedom among the people.

When I say that I know how I cure, people say I blaspheme and make myself equal with Christ. They do not know how I cure and dislike to admit that anyone else does. Consequently they strive to make my explanation as objectionable as possible

Is it a sin to know this and teach it for the happiness of mankind, and do I make myself equal with Christ? If I do then I will submit to the odium willingly.

Aristocracy never complains of oppression except when it cannot oppress. Its motto is "rule or ruin," and where it rules slavery is considered a divine institution. Science is mocked at in its religion and the mockery is echoed by hypocrisy, and it sits in the hearts of the rulers and delivers the law.

The greatest modern philosopher, the missionary doctor admired as one of the true Christians of the twentieth century, the best-known of American physicians, and the priest-scientist known as one of this century's great thinkers – they all experienced the opposition of all opinions:

Anyone who seeks for the true causes of miracles, and strives to understand natural phenomenon as an intelligent being, and not to gaze at them like a fool, is set down and denounced as an impious heretic by those whom the masses adore as the interpreters of nature and the gods. Such persons know that, with the removal of ignorance, the wonder which forms their only available means for proving and preserving their authority would vanish also.

– Benedict de Spinoza – he was excommunicated.

The organized political, social, and religious associations of our time are at work to induce the individual man not to arrive at his convictions by his own thinking but to make his own such convictions as they keep ready-made for him. Any man who thinks for himself and at the same time is spiritually free, is to them something inconvenient and even uncanny.

– Albert Schweitzer, M.D.

Schweitzer was revered as a musician and as a missionary doctor. His admirers conveniently forgot the attacks on him for his studies of the life of Jesus. He knew of the opposition of all opinions.

Three learned professions (medicine, law, and religion) have but recently emerged from a state of barbarism.

Primal instincts are violated when ideas of the healing art, of the administration of justice, of Christian love, could not exclude systematic poisoning, judicial duelling, and murder for opinion's sake.

– Oliver Wendell Holmes, M.D.

Dr. Holmes was condemned – then ignored – when he wrote, before Semelweis, that childbed fever is contagious and carried from woman to woman by physicians.

"Go quietly ahead with your scientific work without getting involved in philosophy or theology . . ."

Throughout my whole life, that is the advice (and the warning) that authority will be found repeatedly to have given me. And such, too, I imagine the directive given to many brilliant youngsters who are now, when the time is so opportune, entering the field of research.

With all respect and yet with the assurance I draw from fifty years spent living in the heart of the problem, I should like to remark to those it properly concerns that it is psychologically unviable and, what is more, directly opposed to the greater glory of God.

– Father Teilhard de Chardin, S.J.

The Jesuit father was prohibited from teaching, exiled to China, and his lifework was barred from publication until after his death.

Part III – Religion

*The effect of impressions made on me
while sitting with the sick.*

Chapter 13

Talking About Religion

My religion is in my acts

It is easier to talk *about* religion than to talk it. To talk it is to put it into practice, and to put it into practice is to give it to those who ask. To give to every one that asks of you some spiritual food or knowledge is not so easy as to sit down and thank the Lord that you are not like other men.

I have no religion independent of my acts. When I am not putting my religion into practice for the benefit of the sick and those I can help, then if I talk I am talking *about* something.

There is a vast difference between talking a theory and talking *about* a theory. Talking about a theory is like talking about a science we do not understand. It contains no wisdom.

As I have the Bible, I have the same means of judging as anyone, for every one has a right to his opinion concerning it. But there is no truth in an opinion unless it can be put into practice as Christ put His into practice, then it becomes a fact.

One of Christ's followers made a remark like this in regard to the same distinction, only he called their talk or belief, Faith, which is religion put in practice. He said, I will show you my religion or faith by my works.*

There is no such identity
as goodness by itself.

Goodness was considered by the priests as a sort of subjection to the rulers. A good person was like a good dog, ready to obey his master; then his master would pat him and call him a good dog, although he had just torn another dog to pieces, or had done something else to please his master.

Religion is what it was before Christ and I think I know what that was. The religion that Christ opposed consisted in forms and ceremonies. Religion makes no compromise, it is rule or ruin. It sometimes takes to itself the name of reform, giving every man the liberty of speech, and then it subjects every one to its laws. This was the way with the Christian church: to be good was to persecute all who would not bow the knee to the leaders. You will see religion in its purest state under the most despotic form of government.

---

* "Even so faith, if it hath not works, is dead, being alone. Yea, a man may say, thou hast faith, and I have works; shew me thy faith without thy works, and I will shew thee my faith by my works."

James 2:17-18 in King James Bible

These lines attributed to the disciple James are troubling to Protestants who prefer the apostle Paul's and Luther's "justification by faith alone."

The practical man, Quimby, preferred "works."

The fact is that religious beliefs are founded in deception and the leaders deceive the people into them. Does the priest call on the people to get understanding? No, that is what he fears. The priests want them to have religion, that is, to believe in the creeds which cramp the intellect and bind burdens upon them so that they can lead them. They fear investigation, for it is death to their craft.

As the priesthood was founded on superstition, it was necessary to keep the people superstitious, so all sorts of inventions were created to keep the people in ignorance. Whatever the prophets could make the people believe, they would create. So all they had to do was to start a storm of evil spirits, and the people's superstition would produce the phenomena wanted. This was proof that evil spirits did exist.

The knowledge of man puts false constructions on his wisdom and gets up a sort of religion which has nothing to do with Jesus' truth. There is where the fault lies. If you do not believe the Bible as they explain it, then you are an infidel. So all who cannot believe it as it has been explained must throw it away.

I do not throw the Bible away, but throw the explanations away, and apply Jesus' own words as He did and as He intended they should be applied, and let my works speak for themselves. My religion, like Jesus', is in my acts not in my belief.

I will give you the trinity that I believe in, that is, P. P. Quimby's trinity. He believes in one living and true wisdom called God, in Jesus – flesh and blood – a medium of this truth, and in the Holy Ghost or explanation of God to man. Here is my trinity and the Holy Ghost is the Science that will lead you all into truth: it will break the bond of error and triumph over the opinion of the world.

Sitting with the Sick

All my writings are the effect of impressions made on me while sitting with the sick, so that my book is of the lives and sufferings of my patients, their trials and sorrows, and my arguments are in their behalf. It may seem strange to the well that I write upon so many subjects, but when you take into consideration the great variety of persons, and the peculiar state of literature, varying from the most cultivated to that of the lowest intellect, it would not be strange if my writings did not excite the curiosity of the reader.

For instance, one is full of religious ideas and becomes almost insane, and some are entirely so. This excites me, and my thoughts run upon religion. Another will be almost insane upon spiritualism; then I have to battle that, or show the absurdity of that belief. Some are excited upon Millerism, and believe the world is coming to an end. This brings up arguments to refute their belief. Some upon witchcraft. Now their minds are continually dwelling on all these subjects and on the Bible. So to cure, I have to show by the Bible that they have been made to believe a false construction. My arguments change their minds and the cure comes. This is my excuse for what I have said upon the Scriptures.

The further the spiritual evolution of mankind advances, the more certain it seems to me that the path to genuine religiosity does not lie through the fear of life, and the fear of death, and blind faith, but through striving after rational knowledge.

– Albert Einstein

After close on two centuries of passionate struggles, neither science nor faith has succeeded in discrediting its adversary. On the contrary, it becomes obvious that neither can develop normally without the other. And the reason is simple: the same life animates both.

Religion and science are the two conjugated faces or phases of one and the same act of complete knowledge – the only one which can embrace the past and future of evolution so as to contemplate, measure and fulfill them.

– Teilhard de Chardin

Christianity cannot take the place of thinking, but it must be founded on it.

The man who thinks stands up freer in the face of traditional religious truth than the man who does not, but the profound and imperishable elements contained in it he assimilates with much more effect than the latter.

I think the most important quality in a person concerned with religion is absolute devotion to the truth.

– Albert Schweitzer

Photographic copy of one of the few pages of Quimby's notes printed as an appendix in the 1921 edition of The Quimby Manuscripts. Similar copies are in the 1961 edition.

Chapter 14

If Jesus Should Appear

That unseen principle

Jesus taught, and His teaching was the healing of nations.

If His Truth had not been misconstrued, the world at this time would have been rid of thousands of errors it now has.

Eighteen hundred years ago, there was a man called Jesus who, the Christian says, came from heaven to tell man that if he would conform to certain rules and regulations he could go to heaven when he died; but if he refused to obey them he must go to hell.

If Jesus should appear on earth and could hear the explanations given to his remarks which he made eighteen hundred years ago, He never would imagine that He was in any way alluded to.

All religion that embraces creeds is of this world, and is governed by laws, and contains rewards and punishments, therefore holding out inducements to be good with one hand, and retribution with the other, is not the religion of Christ.

He is in us, and a part of us, and to know ourselves is to know Christ, and to preach Christ is to help each other out of our troubles, destroying the enemy that has possession of us.

Christ is that unseen principle in man of which man is conscious, but which he has never considered as intelligence. It is God in us, and when man comes to recognize it as intelligence transcending belief and learns its principles, then death will be swallowed in Wisdom.

Jesus taught Christ and put it in practice by His words. Do the Christians the same? No, they preach *about* it. To talk wisdom is wisdom, whereas to talk *about* wisdom is to talk an unknown God.

If you claim to be a good man and we see no proof of your goodness on others, your goodness is of this world, not of Christ. To be a follower of Jesus and believer in the Christ is to separate yourself from the world and stand alone in your wisdom.

To be a follower of Christ is to do things that He did, but to be a *believer* in Christ only embraces what you know nothing of only as a belief. Jesus was called the Son of God. To be a Son of God you must do His will, and His will is to subject your errors to the Truth.

At the time of Jesus the world was in darkness in regard to man's future state. Society was divided into sects, and priests by their craft ruled the masses and kept them in bondage, constantly frightening them with what would come after death.

Lucretius, who lived one hundred and fifty years before Christ, gives a true account of the religion of his day, which could not have varied much from that of the time of Jesus. I will quote an extract from his poem. After describing the horrors of religion, he says:

"But still I fear your caution will dispute
  the maxims I lay down
Who all your life have troubled
  at the poet's frightful tales.
Alas, I could even now invent such dreams
  as would pervert the strictest rules of
  reason and make your fortunes tumble
  to the bottom.
No words but if man were once convinced that
  death was the sure end of all their pains,
They might with reason resist the force
  of all religion, and condemn the threats
  of priests,
Now we have no sense, no power to strive
  against these prejudices because we fear
  a scene of endless torment after death."

To suppose that Jesus taught any such religion as is here referred to, is to put him on a level with the priests. Opposition to the popular religion was sure death and he was forced to come in conflict with it.

> The reader, seeing the quoting of Lucretius, may need to be reminded that these and all other words in this book, except as plainly marked or obvious, are the writings of P. P. Quimby. He was a self-educated but well-educated man.

Jesus Christ belonged to the true race of prophets....He said,..."I am divine. Through me, God acts; through me, speaks. Would you see God, see me; or see thee, when though also thinkest as I now think." But what a distortion did his doctrine and memory suffer in the same, in the next, and the following ages!

— Ralph Waldo Emerson

If we Christians wish to retain in Christ the very qualities on which his power and our worship are based, we have no better way – no other way, even – of doing so than fully to accept the most modern concepts of evolution. Under the combined pressure of science and philosophy, we are being forced, experientially and intellectually, to accept the world as a coordinated system of activity which is gradually rising up toward freedom and consciousness.

— Father Teilhard de Chardin

Jesus does not think dogmatically. He formulates no doctrine. He is far from judging any man's belief by reference to any standard of dogmatic correctness. Nowhere does he demand of His hearers that they shall sacrifice thinking to believing....I am certain that truthfulness in all things belongs to the spirit of Jesus.

— Albert Schweitzer

Miracles do not happen in contradiction to nature, but only in contradiction to that which is known to us of nature.

— Saint Augustine

Chapter 15

True Prayer

The desire of the heart

I have no account with God,
He pays me as soon as my work is done.
I do not ask favors of Him
  apart from his principles.
If I act wrongly
  He will not step out and correct me.
I must do it myself.

God rewards everyone according to his acts, and He knows our wants before we ask. To ask of a Being whom we acknowledge knows our wants is either to curry favor or flatter Him with the idea that we think He will be pleased to see how much we honor Him.

This is the wisdom of this world, but not the wisdom of God. God asks no such worship.

He who expects God to leave Science and come down to ignorance and change a principle for a selfish motive to please him is either a knave or fool and knows not God.

All people pray to a being independent of themselves, acknowledging a state or place where God is, and when they pray, supposing that He listens, ask Him to hear prayers and relieve their wants. This is precisely what the heathen did, and Jesus called them hypocrites and condemned them, for He said this offering up of prayer and sacrifices year after year could never take away sin or error.

Can any good come out of prayer? I answer "yes" but not in the sense that is supposed. A phenomenon can be produced in the same way that is brought about by mesmerism, but there is no knowledge in the church-prayer. It is the effect of superstition and ignorance. It is not of Christ, but from a mind ignorant of self and God. No man prays except the one who wants a favor, to be rewarded for more than he deserves, or one who has more of this world's goods than his neighbor.

No man of character will beg or pray
for the sake of gain.

True prayer is the desire of the heart,
and if the heart is right
the prayer will be answered.

A true heart must have scientific knowledge, and a corrupt heart must be full of superstition and ignorance, deceit and hypocrisy.

I look on church-prayers as I do on all other errors that have been invented to govern mankind and keep the people in ignorance of themselves and God.

Prayer is the law of man, not of God, and makes God nothing but a mere sorcerer or magician to frighten the ignorant and superstitious.

We are taught to believe that if we pray, we shall receive an answer to our prayer. A superstitious person believing this is ready to believe that he may be punished, for some one may pray that God may remove him.

The priests would offer up prayers to their God for the salvation of souls, and the doctors would offer up prayers for their business.

Each army prays that God will direct the weapons that will slay their enemies.

Jesus said, *"Not all who say Lord! Lord! shall enter into this theory or kingdom, but he that doeth the will of the Father that sent him."*

A prayer made up of words is lost unless accompanied by good to some one, and if we do good to one another our prayer is in the act.

True prayer is in our acts. False prayer is in our words, and by their fruits you shall know them.

Ralph Waldo Emerson had this to say about prayer:

Prayer is the contemplation of the facts of life from the highest point of view. It is the soliloquy of a beholding and jubilant soul. It is the spirit of God pronouncing his work good. . . . Prayer that craves a particular commodity, anything less than all good, is vicious. . . . Prayer as a means to effect a private end is meanness and theft.

Voltaire replied to a report of the saving of a sparrow by prayer:

I believe in a general Providence which has laid down for all eternity the law which governs all things, like light from the sun; but I believe not that a particular Providence changes the economy of the world for your sparrow.

Father Teilhard de Chardin believed this about miracles:

Personally, I have no difficulty in accepting miracles, providing (and this, in fact, is precisely what the church teaches) the miracle does not run counter to the continually more numerous and exact rules we are finding in the natural evolution of the world. (In fact, taking even the gospel marvels in the form they are often presented in, I feel obliged to admit that I believe not because of but in spite of the miracles I am offered. And I am sure that is the unacknowledged position of a great many Christians.)

Chapter 16

There is No Good in Dying

Our next world is here

I use words merely for convenience which I say are wrong, for example: "death." The time will come when such words will be obsolete. They will not be used when there is knowledge.

Every person who was, or ever will be, existed as much before he ever came to our senses as afterwards, the same as any mathematical truth.

When the senses shall be attached to this Wisdom, then shall be brought to pass that saying:

"Oh! death! where is thy sting!
Oh, grave! where is thy victory!"
Death is robbed of its victim.
The grave gives up its idea of death.

It is a common remark that after we shake off this mortal coil the spirit will be set free. This is to acknowledge that the body is larger than the spirit or wisdom. No wonder with such a belief men pray to be delivered from the body of sin and death.

The fact is that the theory of the body and soul is not in keeping with the progress of truth or science. It leaves everything in the dark. It gives no proof of any phenomenon.

You see how all those persons that can work themselves up to believe that the time is coming when our bodies will rise again are about as far behind the times as those old persons who believe the time will come when the factories will be abolished and the girls will return to the spinning wheel and loom, when steam will be abolished. If they can get any comfort out of that kind of food, I for one will not disturb their repose.

Man has to get up a belief in opposition to the Bible's belief. He must believe Jesus went to heaven with a body of flesh and blood. This upset what Jesus intended to prove, that is, that although they should destroy this flesh and blood, Christ would show Himself to prove that man can live and have all his faculties and knowledge after the world calls him dead.

Man is always dying and living
  in progression,
For error or opinion
  must always be in the mind
And mind must always exist
  till time is no more.

There is no good in dying.
For that does not change us at all.

If you want the satisfaction of having friends with you, never hint that they are going away for you will drive them from you, but sit by them just as though you were all together and you will see a scene that you will always greatly remember, for you will always feel this life of your friend or child mingling with yours, not to be separated by a belief.

The religious people of Jesus' day, like the Christians of this day, made heaven and hell places independent of man. The priests tell their hearers there is another world separate from this. They give such a glowing account of it that their opinions, like fuel, set fire to the audience and a chemical change takes place; their minds are disturbed and their senses are affected by the opinions of the priests.

An expedition is fitted out to go to this world, which is actually created by the priests' opinions. The locality of this world is a mystery, so all varieties of speculation are got up about it.

The natural man, being superstitious and ignorant, is easily led by the cunning errors of the world. The leaders, being crafty and superstitious, believe in every phonemenon which is produced, and they attribute it to a power from the invisible world.

Our next world is here where we are and always must be. This teaches us to do to others as we would have others do to us, because *we are all a part of each other.*

When we injure one part, the whole feels it.

Death and heaven have been the subjects of a long search and diverse findings. The seventeenth-century lens grinder in Holland and the twentieth-century teacher from India have made these reports:

As there is something which is conceived by a certain eternal necessity through the very essence of God; this something, which appertains to the essence of the mind, will necessarily be eternal.

Those are far astray from a true estimate of virtue who expect for their virtue, as if it were the greatest slavery, that God will adorn them with the greatest rewards; as if virtue and the serving of God were not happiness itself and the greatest liberty.

– Benedict de Spinoza

Do you know what it means to die, not physically, but psychologically, inwardly?

You can't say to death, let me finish my job, let me finish my book, all the things I have not done, let me heal the hurts which I have given others. You have no time.

So can you find out how to live a life now, today, in which there is always an ending to everything that you began?

One has to find out for oneself what it means to die; then there is no fear, therefore every day is a new day – and I really mean this, one CAN do this – so that your mind and your eyes see life as something totally new. That is eternity.

– J. Krishnamurti

Part IV – Thoughts

The poor soldier . . .
Love . . .
The life of woman . . .

Chapter 17

The Poor Soldier

A crown of glory awaits

The poor soldier who fights for the leaders sinks under the burden bound upon him. To keep up his courage, the officers hold up the idea he is fighting for a great and good cause. And a crown of glory in heaven awaits those who die upon the battlefield. This is all the happiness the privates get. So they fight to keep society from ruin while their reward is the satisfaction of fighting the devil and supporting the officers.

Reverse the tables, making the priest the soldier, tax him to pay the former soldier for his instructions. Then it would be shown how well their principle of action, which they preach to others, applies to themselves.

Jesus saw through all this hypocrisy: that the God of the heathen was not the God of peace, but of war, and this same God is worshipped now as then. He is the most convenient God I know of. He listens to the North and the South and leads their men on to battle and from the prayers of his followers is as much interested in the victory as the winning party. All this sort of cant is kept up with a certain solemnity of form as though there were real truth in it. But the time will come when all this must give way to a higher worship.

The Search for Truth

Let us stop to think for a moment of the proportion of human energy devoted, here and now, to the pursuit of truth. Or, in still more concrete terms, let us glance at the percentage of a nation's revenue allotted in its budget for the investigation of clearly-defined problems whose solution would be of vital consequence for the world. If we did we should be staggered. Less is provided annually for all the pure research all over the world than for one capital ship. Surely our great-grandsons will not be wrong if they think of us as barbarians?

Father Teilhard de Chardin, S.J.

Do you also want to end all wars as I do? Do you understand? It means no nationality, no frontiers, no linguistic differences, no religious divisions – all that. No, Sir, you can't demonstrate, you have to live it. And when you live it, that in itself is a demonstration.

– J. Krishnamurti

Chapter 18

Love

The power wisdom uses

Love is an element of itself,
without any form.
It has no length or breadth,
or height or depth.

It neither comes nor goes.
It fills all space.
And melts all error down
that comes within its power.

What is the element that receives all sensation? Love for ourselves. This is the ground work or foundation of all our acts. It is the mortar dough in which all sensation is made. Of itself it contains no knowledge.

It is perfect harmony; its elements or language is its perfection. It embraces all the senses; it is not Wisdom but the power Wisdom uses to bring all things into harmony with itself.

You see a person, at first sight you are affected, and you attach your senses to the idea in the form of love. You may or may not be deceived. Passion or excitement is matter governed by error acting upon ignorance. Science is to keep the two separate or in subjection to Wisdom.

A child knows its mother, not by looks, but by something not included within these two senses: it is that something that makes her different in her relation to the child from any other woman. Suppose it be called love, or a desire for the child's happiness identified with her own.

According as she directs the child in the pure intelligence of that love or shields her feelings to knowledge derived from a source which does not contain that love, so shall the fruits be.

This love contains an intelligence which if followed in spirit and truth may destroy every obstacle in the way of the child's happiness, and develop it into a self-governing responsible being. Then why is it not so?

Because from our religious and social education no woman can carry out the high principle of her affection. She is taught by established morality to put restrictions on the child that would make her miserable in the child's place.

The laws of love are the destruction
  of the laws of error,
And they make us a law to ourselves.

Love is a substance like food
  that comes from heaven to feed the soul.

Chapter 19

The Life of Woman

The spiritual rib

As the soil of California
  is rich enough to produce gold,
So the soul or life of the female
  is rich enough to produce the Wisdom of God.
The life of woman contains
  more spiritual wisdom than is found in man.

Women have more
  of the scientific element,
Less of the animal.
Man partakes more of the animal,
  less of the scientific.

Women have more endurance
  and more patience
  to investigate any new science.
And their wisdom is not of this world,
  but of that higher power called Science.

But a female coming forward in public
  to advocate man's ideas
Is as much below the male
  as a male who personifies a brute
  for the gratification of an audience
  is below the brute itself.

The male creation
 feeds on the lower order of life.
It makes the higher order
 a sort of pet for a while.
The natural man sports and plays
 with the female.

But man from some cause, probably from having more physical strength, and looking upon all things as inferior to his own wisdom, is not content to subject all the brute creation to his will, but must subject the very creature that his best life or nature adores, and in this way woman is deprived of carrying out the science that God intended.

Now where is woman placed? Just where man puts her to satisfy himself. She has nothing to do with her situation, but she must be content with what man chooses to assign her.

Where is woman's true position? As a teacher of the Science of Health and Happiness. This is what man does not want to do. It is too much like labor to toil over little children, and sit by the sick and take their sufferings upon oneself.

The spiritual rib that rises from man is more perfect matter or soil, called "woman." I do not mean that "woman" means every female. Nor do I pretend to say that "man" means everything of the animal, but that the mind of the female contains more of that superior substance required to receive the higher development of God's Wisdom. For this element is pure love that has been purified by the change life has gone through.

The identity of woman's soul can be compared to a fire, which throws an equal heat all around. This heat is pure love, containing no knowledge, no selfishness, but is like the love of a mother for her child.

One of Doctor Quimby's women patients, an intensely interested student of his science, was Mrs. Mary M. Patterson, known as Mary Baker Eddy, founder of the Christian Science church. She published this sonnet in the Lynn, Massachusetts, newspaper in 1866:

"Lines on the death of Dr. P.P. Quimby, who healed with the truth that Christ taught, in contradistinction to all isms.

Did sackcloth clothe the sun, and day grow night,
All matter mourn the hour with dewy eyes,
When Truth, receding from our mortal sight,
Had paid to error her last sacrifice?
Can we forget the power that gave us life?
Shall we forget the wisdom of its way?
Then ask me not, amid this mortal strife, –
This keenest pang of animated, clay, –
To mourn him less: to mourn him more were just,
If to his memory 'twere a tribute given
For every solemn, sacred, earnest trust
Delivered to us ere he rose to heaven.
Heaven but the happiness of that calm soul,
Growing in stature to the throne of God:
Rest should reward him who hath made us whole,
Seeking, though tremblers,
where his footsteps trod."

The Search for Truth

Someone will ask whether women are under men's authority by nature or institution? For if it has been by mere institution, then we had no reason compelling us to exclude women from government. But if we consult experience itself, we shall find that the origin of it is in their weakness. For there has never been a case of men and women reigning together, but see that men rule, and women are ruled, and that on this plan, both sexes live in harmony. One may assert with perfect propriety, that women have not by nature equal right with men: but necessarily give way to men, and thus it cannot happen, that both sexes should rule alike, much less that men should be ruled by women.

– Benedict de Spinoza, 1660

But this is a truth: A belief may be changed

– P. P. Quimby, 1860

These Ideas

An Epilogue

I know I am writing this
 if I know anything,
But to know that I shall finish it
 admits a doubt.
To know that you will understand it
 admits more doubt.

Now to remind you of what I tried
 to make you understand
 is a very hard task on my part;
For some of my ideas
 fall on stony ground,
 and some on dry ground,
 and some on good ground.

These ideas are in your mind
 like little leaven.
They will work
 till the whole mind is changed.

Doctor P. P. Quimby and His World

Phineas Parkhurst Quimby was born in New Hampshire, February 16, 1802. His labor ended on January 16, 1866. Quimby intended to put his wisdom into a book, but did not have the time. His wisdom lives on.

The reader may wish to recall that in 1860 formal medical practice was mostly useless and often harmful. Doctor Quimby's opinion of the "medical faculty" was harsh but realistic. Compare his words with those of one of the most eminent medical men of his day, a professor of medicine at Harvard:

I have observed the effect of medicine and found that there is more virtue or misery in the advertisement than in the medicine.

P. P. Quimby
Self-educated healer, 1862

I firmly believe that if the whole materia medica, as now used, could be sunk to the bottom of the sea it would be all the better for mankind and all the worse for the fishes.

Professor Oliver Wendell Holmes, M.D.
Harvard University Medical School, 1860

In 1843, Holmes published a paper warning that child-bed fever is contagious. The medical men scoffed and ignored his warning.

In 1844, Ignace Semmelweis entered an obstetric ward to begin his campaign to save women from this hospital holocaust. It was not until 1864 that Pasteur announced the proof of "germs" in the air carrying infection.

Doctor Quimby's last notes are dated July 15, 1865.

On August 17, 1865, Doctor Semmelweis, frustrated by more than fifteen years of futile effort to get obstetricians and surgeons to wash their hands, stabbed himself in the hand with a contaminated scalpel. His death of infection was his final offer of proof of his wisdom. Lister applied this knowledge to surgery in 1865 but said, "Without Semmelweis my achievements would be nothing."

Medication in 1865 could best be described as "grotesque" (I went to the Stanford medical archives and read some of it.). Surgeons washed after surgery, not before. But the medical faculty was not the only source of disease and death.

Not only did the medical faculty do physical harm with abominable medications and filthy surgery, they also did mental harm. The medical men commonly aggravated their patients' problems by evil suggestions. Frightening diagnoses without real merit often caused the disease. As Doctor Quimby tells us: "You tell me I look sick . . . at last I die . . . this is disease. And you made it."

Calvinistic religion was strong in New England. Doctor Quimby refers to "Calvinist Baptists." From the pulpit, patients were told they were being rightly punished by a vengeful God who invented these tortures for the sinful humans He had created. Unable to recall how they had sinned and imagining sins never committed, or inventing sins to fit the disease, they suffered helplessly.

Unlike small-pox, this disease of the religious mind has not been vanquished. In 2006, an American religious leader said that Israel Prime Minister Sharon's brain hemorrhage was God's divine retribution for Sharon's giving up a part of the God's promised land in an effort to achieve peace. A vengeful God indeed.

Puritan theology "was more likely to cause a fever than to mention one," said Oliver Wendell Holmes in 1836. The following year, P. P. Quimby began his research. In seven years - near the end of his notes - he treated more than twelve thousand different persons. People came, riding in buggies and wagons for hundreds of miles, to stay in the International Hotel near Quimby's office and be helped by the man they called "Doctor."

Doctor Quimby blamed the medical faculty for the invention of fad diseases, including "falling of the womb, internal ulcers, ovarian tumors, weak spine, heart disease, neuralgia, and spine disease." There is no doubt that many of these diagnoses given to Quimby's patients long before the invention of X-rays were false and frightening.

In all fairness to the medical men of 1865, the incidence of false treatment was not so greatly higher than it is today. In modern times we know of unjustified tonsillectomies, hysterectomies, sleep drugs, tranquilizers, stimulants, drugging of "hyperactive" children, and other fads of the profession. But there is growing awareness among enlightened medical men and women that P. P. Quimby, whom they do not know, was right more often than not.

The medical establishment now acknowledges a continuously growing list of complaints under the influence or control of the mind, including peptic ulcer, colitis, bronchial asthma, dermatitis, hay fever, urticaria, angio-neurotic edema, arthritis, Raynaud's disease, hypertension, hyperthyroidism, amenorrhea, enuresis, paroxysmal tachycardia, migraine headache, impotence, alcoholism, hysteria, neurasthenia, and respiratory diseases including tuberculosis (consumption), cerebral infarction, warts, diabetes, Parkinsonism, angina pectoris, allergies, skin diseases, insomnia, multiple sclerosis, menopausal disturbances, and a wide variety of neuroses. Medical journals add to the list every month.

A recent poll of physicians elicited opinions that from fifty percent to eighty percent of persons first arriving at a doctor's office come with a psychosomatic complaint. Certainly, many of Quimby's patients suffered from hysteria, that strange affliction named after the womb. His most famous patient was an outstanding example, who with strong will lived to nearly ninety.

As Quimby started his notes after years of healing, in 1859 in France, Paul Briquet published his *Treatise on Hysteria*. This thorough study stands scrutiny against the best modern standards of research. Briquet found one-quarter of the female patients in a hospital to have hysteria and another quarter to be "very impressionable." There were twenty times more women than men hysterics in another group he studied.

Briquet quoted from the standard medical text, written in 1694, still in use in 1859, by Sydenham:

> "Amongst women, there exists a more lively sensitiveness than among men. Feelings are more easily aroused, are experienced more intensely, and have more repercussions in the whole economy than amongst men."

Briquet observed, "These characteristics were in keeping with the social and biological needs of women and were the reason why hysteria was so much more prevalent in women than in men." In Briquet's words:

> "No illness is more difficult to cure . . . half recover only when advancing age dulls their sensitivities . . . Some . . . are condemned to a lifetime of suffering, malaise, and sometimes serious illness. They may spend a year or more in bed, completely incapacitated . . . old before their time, leading a wretched life for themselves and those around them."

There is now a move to rename "hysteria" by calling it "Briquet's syndrome." But his superb study had not been translated into English. The all-male medical faculty had not cared enough about this affliction they associated with the womb.

Doctor Quimby cared. Phineas Parkhuurst Quimby, called "Doctor" by his grateful patients, a clock-maker and inventor of mechanical devices became America's greatest healer. He learned the wisdom of the ages by sitting with sorely afflicted people, listening to their false beliefs, and instructing them so they would heal themselves.

Park Quimby entered his career as a healer through the study and demonstration of mesmerism. A true scientist, he experimented and observed. He rejected mesmerism for healing as a deception, but these experiments and his later studies taught him the true nature of disease and the true method of healing.

Doctor Quimby's main concern throughout is with the problem of false beliefs. All that he writes has to do with this problem. He expresses his own beliefs mainly to show that change is possible and to compel his patients and you, the readers, to analyze their beliefs. This, he says, is the greatest study of all.

He found that beliefs create disease. He healed by showing the errors. His cures were in his belief or wisdom. He tells us that truth is the cure. He found medical cures to be, not in the medicine but in the confidence of the doctor. Great medical men have said the same. Many successful drugs, prescribed in great quantity, have been later found to be no more than placebos "given to please" but without material effect, yet effective in curing.

Doctor Quimby had clairvoyant ability, which he explains. He had the ability to "clearly see" – to clearly sense – the feelings of his patients; and to such a degree as to become two persons at once: himself and a person with the feelings of his patient. The feelings were so real as to be sometimes frightening. It was this great power of empathy, coupled with his analysis of false beliefs, that made him a miraculous healer.

Doctor Quimby did not claim to heal every affliction. Sweeping claims of perfect solutions to all ills are the province of charlatans and religious cults. In a circular sent to those people who wrote for information, he advised:

If any person is nearly gone with consumption, I should advise him to stay at home unless it is to be relieved of the distress, so it is with a great many kinds of disease.

Treatment by Doctor Quimby varied in length, from one visit to many visits, and was often followed up by correspondence. Quimby wrote to reply to patients' questions and remind them of what he had taught them. He wrote with encouragement and with the offer of "absent treatment":

I wish now to let you know that I am still with you, sitting by you while you are in bed, encouraging you to keep up good spirits and all will go right.

He did not accept payment if he could not help. As a craftsman and inventor, he could earn his living without healing, but chose the hard course of healing against the resistance of the medical faculty and the religious faculty. He felt called to do this work. No one ever accused Doctor Quimby of profiteering. No one ever doubted his sincerity. And there is no doubt that he helped thousands of sick people.

We know how Doctor Quimby came to so much wisdom. He tells us – both in his Introductions and throughout his notes. He was a scientist. He observed people. He learned from them. He was not burdened by dogmas of medical schools or theologies, by the empty words of politicians or by the rules of the aristocrats.

Doctor Quimby mentions sympathy as something he supplied his patients, but it is obvious that he often made it clear that he was not in sympathy with their beliefs. He never used the word "empathy" – a new word not appearing until 1904 – but "empathy" describes his method.

Quimby so strongly sensed the feelings of his patients that these sometimes frightened him. It was only by the exercise of will and wisdom that he was able to avoid taking on the diseases of his patients. This is a problem reported by all empathic healers. From time to time he found it necessary to leave Portland for a few day's rest.

After consultation, and sometimes during such a session, he would go to his office and add to his notes. Two sisters, Emma and Sarah Ware – daughters of a United States Supreme Court Justice – or his son, George Quimby, would make copies of his notes and suggest minor corrections.

Some of Doctor Quimby's patients were also his students and confidants. Although he never organized a clinic or church and his book was not completed, there are today many churches, healing groups, and self-improvement organizations that are lineal descendants of the teaching of P. P. Quimby. Some of those are now loosely affiliated by the International New Thought Alliance, but others are unaware of their debt to Phineas Parkhurst Quimby.

The wisdom of Quimby is universal, but few have fully learned its lessons. Doctor Quimby was the first to teach what is now popularly called "positive thinking." But he discovered much more while sitting with thousands of sorely troubled people. He discovered a philosophy of life, an enlightened religion, and the existence of clairvoyant relations among persons.

After twenty years of healing practice in Portland and Belfast, Maine, he began to write notes recording his observations and his knowledge for an intended book. His notes are a daily journal: repetitive and disorganized. He did not have time to edit the notes and the book never was published. We have his notes preserved in the Library of Congress. Three compilations have been published.

Because his notes were not published until sixty years after his death – and then disorganized, incomplete, and difficult to read – Quimby is little known even to those who acknowledge him as the origin of their beliefs. It is the purpose of this book to make the wisdom of Park Quimby more available.

"Only from the authors themselves can we receive philosophic thoughts; therefore whoever feels drawn to philosophy must seek out its immortal teachers in the still sanctuary of their own works."

We follow this advice of the philosopher Arthur Schopenhauer in seeking out the wisdom of Park Quimby in his own words. But the words of one teacher, however great, are only selected fruits from the tree of Wisdom. We will all know the tree better if we learn also from many teachers. But how to distinguish fruits of the tree of Wisdom from the fruits of the tree of false beliefs which is so much more prolific? The missionary doctor, Albert Schweitzer tells us:

"Just as a tree bears year after year the same fruit and yet fruit which is each year new, so must all permanently valuable ideas be continually born again in thought."

We see the validity of Doctor Quimby's opinions by the fact that they have been discovered and rediscovered by great thinkers in all nations and cultures and from all ages. Quimby expresses them in simple words written in his office while sitting with patients.

Doctor Quimby wrote:

"Make man responsible for his beliefs and he will be as cautious in what he believes as he is in what he sees or does."

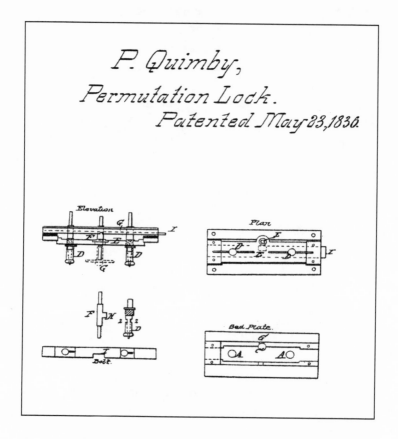

P. P. Quimby was – above all – a practical man. A clockmaker and inventor he studied mesmerism for four years and learned that *"what we believe, we create."* Finding that mesmerism was unnecessary and even deceptive, he rejected it. He spent the next twenty years studying and practicing healing. He then began to write the notes of which this book is a sample. He was the first modern man to *"unlock the secret which has been a mystery for ages to mankind."*

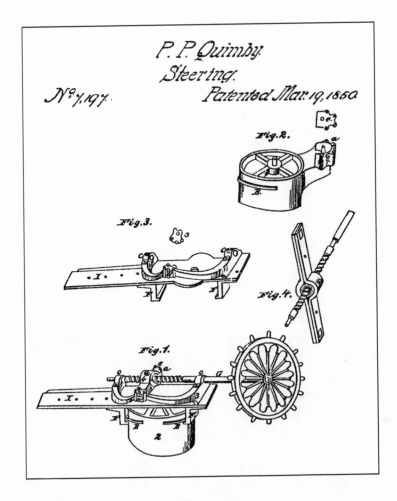

Quimby held these four patents:
  Improvement in machine for cutting panels,
    dated September 12, 1829; with Job White.
  Chain saw for timber etc. June 3, 1829.
  (those two were lost in the Patent Office fire of 1836)
  Permutation lock. May 23, 1836
  Steering apparatus. March 19, 1850.

Bibliography

The most important Quimby source is the three-volume set compiled by Dr. Ervin Seale as his retirement task:

The *Complete Writings of Phineas Parkhurst Quimby* edited by Dr. Ervin Seale; 1988; three volumes. ISBN: 0-87516-600-8 Publisher: DeVorss & Company; Marina del Rey, California.

Seale's work had not yet been published at the time this collection in your hand was compiled.

The Quimby manuscripts themselves are now in the Library of Congress. Some libraries may have microfilm copies.

―――――――――

The sources for the quotations in this book, *The Healing Wisdom of Dr. P. P. Quimby*, were three:

The Quimby Manuscripts; Showing the Discovery of Spiritual Healing and the Origin of Christian Science, Edited by Horatio W. Dresser; 1921, Thomas Y. Crowell; New York.

This is the original publication of Quimby's notes, edited by the son of Julius and Annetta Dresser, patients and students of Dr. Quimby. It is long out of print, but found in some libraries (mine came from the California State Library). This large book contains 125,000 words in selections from the manuscripts, with editorial comments and explanations. Included are some 100 pages of history of Quimby. It is now available on the Internet – see Internet references on page 122.

The Quimby Manuscripts. Edited by Horatio W. Dresser with an introduction by Ervin Seale; 1961, Citadel Press, Lyle Stuart; Secaucus, New Jersey. This edition is a photographic reprint of the 1921 book but – by demand of the Christian Science church – omits fourteen letters from Mary Baker Patterson (Eddy) to Dr. Quimby. The excellent introduction by Dr. Ervin Seale summarizes the history and contribution of Quimby.

The Unpublished Writings of Phineas Parkhurst Quimby. Compiled by Erroll S. Collie from the original manuscripts in the Library of congress; 1943, reprinted in 1981. This closely typed, mimeographed transcription contains 200,000 words from the manuscripts not included in the Dresser edition. I was lucky to get a copy.

———————————

The following were not sources of quotations of Quimby but were supporting literature.

Quimby's Science of Happiness; A Non-medical Scientific Explanation of the Cause and Cure of Disease. By Erroll Stafford Collie; 1980. An explanation of Dr. Quimby's teachings by the man who transcribed and made available so much of Quimby's manuscripts. Includes information of newer discoveries in the science of healing.

Phineas Parkhurst Quimby, Revealer of Spiritual Healing to His Age; His Life and What He Taught. By Ann Ballew Hawkins; 1951, Has many biblical references in support of Doctor Quimby's wisdom.

The True History of Mental Science; A Lecture Delivered at the Church of Divine Unity, Boston, Massachusetts, on Sunday evening, February 7, 1887 by Julius Dresser. At this date, this may be found on the internet at: www.ppquimby.com . An eyewitness report by a patient of Doctor Quimby, who was also a student and assistant to the doctor, Dresser gives the history of the development of Quimby's science, describes the man and his work, and quotes the testimonials written by Mary Baker Eddy as well as brief excerpts from Quimby's notes, which were then safeguarded by Doctor Quimby's son.

Spirits in Rebellion; the Rise and Development of New Thought, By Charles S. Braden; 1963, Southern Methodist University Press; Dallas, Texas
Gives the history of the New Thought movement, from Park Quimby to 1963. This is a detailed and unbiased account. ("Bias" is in the eye of the beholder. The history of New Thought is complex and diverse. From Quimby and other historical sources – some of them ancient – various threads of thought have followed.)

The Positive Thinkers; A Study of the American Quest for Health, Wealth and Personal Power from Mary Baker Eddy to Norman Vincent Peale. By Donald Meyer; 1965, Doubleday and Company, Garden City, New York.
Briefly describes the origination by Quimby, then follows the development, not toward New Thought and healing, but toward the more self-centered positive thinking and get-rich popular publications and leaders. This is a comprehensive commentary only within that bound – and tinged with cynicism
It was when looking for the source of "get-rich, positive thinking" that the I stumbled upon this book on the library

shelves and opened it to the first page to find the origin: P. P. Quimby. The publisher apparently chose to use "Mary Baker Eddy" in the title as a more saleable product than the unknown Quimby. That "brief encounter" led to the self-publication of this book when I could find no well-organized, readable publication of Quimby's wisdom.

The Search for Truth encompasses the entire library. Only a trace of that search is given here:

Aurelius, Marcus
Meditations, 180 A.D.; notes of a Roman Emperor.

Einstein – *Albert Out of My Later Years, 1956.*

Emerson, Ralph Waldo – Especially the Harvard Divinity School address of July 1838.

Krishnamurti, J. – *The Awakening of Intelligence, 1973,* and many other books.

Plato – *The Republic*, Book VII, 400 B.C.
This is the shadows-in-the-cave story.

Rogers, Carl – *A Way of Being, 1980; On Becoming a Person; Client-Centered Therapy*; and other books. A modern healer tells how his theories and practice changed while sitting with patients.

Schweitzer, Albert – *Out of My life and Thought*, 1931, written at his hospital in Lambarene, French Equatorial Africa (now the Republic of Gabon).

Spinoza, Benedict de – *Ethics and A Theologico-Politico Treatise*, 1670. Lengthy, detailed, but with many pages that are eminently readable and important.

Teilhard de Chardin – *The Phenomenom of Man, 1930 but published after his death in 1955,* is his masterwork, but numerous smaller books have been published since the death of this long-silenced Jesuit priest-scientist.

The Internet, September 2008, has many pages of New Thought, Quimby, and related material. Unlike paper books and libraries, these are variable from day to day. Here are a few links active today. A search of the internet for others may easily be made. Only the International New Thought Alliance specifically acknowledges Quimby as "founding father." Many other organizations are traceable directly or indirectly to Quimby.

Quimby:

www.ppquimby.com/
phineasquimby.wwwhubs.com/
www.websyte.com/alan/Quimby.htm

New Thought:

www.newthoughtalliance.org/   (the INTA)
websyte.com/alan/
en.wikipedia.org/wiki/New_Thought

1
2
3
4
5
6
7
8
9
10
11
12
13
14
15
16
17
18
19
20
21
22
23
24
25
26
27
28
29
30
31
32
33
34

The Editor

Mason A. Clark, is a physicist and engineer and was a manager of device development in the semiconductor industry. A graduate of the electrical engineering and physics departments of Northwestern University, he was a supervisor of transistor development at the Bell telephone Laboratories, the manager of semiconductor product development for subsidiary companies of the Thompson Ramo Woolridge and Hewlett-Packard corporations, a Vice-President of Microwave Associates West, and in semi-retirement a local sales manager for the Micromanipulator Company, a semiconductor equipment company.

His web site: http://frontal-lobe.info

Concordance – Sources of Quotations

References are to either the Dresser or Collie editions. The relatively few Collie references are marked with a "C". For the Dresser edition the page numbers refer to the 1961 republication by Citadel Press, Lyle Stuart, a photographic copy of the 1921 edition. To refer to the 1921 edition, subtract 6 from the page numbers that are less than 165.

The references were carefully checked. In doing so several points came to the editor's attention. First: the number of superbly phrased and meaningful lines of Quimby that were not used. Several editions of this could be made without using any line twice, so voluminous and redundant was Quimby's daily journal, and with no loss of poetry or meaning. The editor regrets being unable to use them all.

Second: in the third line of the third paragraph on page 30 there appears the phrase "not of talk but of works." In the Dresser edition, second line on page 244, from which this was taken, the phrase is printed as "not of talk but of *words*." Knowing Quimby's wisdom about words versus acts, he would not have written this. Dr. Seale kindly sent a photocopy of Quimby's manuscript showing plainly that Quimby wrote "works."

Finally, the reader should he aware of a difficulty in reading Quimby. He frequently recites a belief of the world without using quotation marks or otherwise indicating that this belief is not his own. They may too easily he mistaken as statements of his own belief unless the reader has studied Quimby enough to know what he intended.

The line numbers in this book are line positions on the page from 1 to 33 (see page 123).

| Healing Wisdom | | Source | Healing Wisdom |
Page	Line	Page	Quotation begins:
8	9	230	In introducing this
	17	415	I fitted out my
9	1	230	My practice for
	5	60	My object in
	16	282	I ran against a
	26	61	If I really believed
	29	71	The reader will find
10	11	72	To cure them was
	21	61	I have said many things
	24	178	My writings are not to
	28	62	The science of curing
11	1	277	Within the last seven
	6	127	It is not a very easy
	27	387	Here you see the true
12	1	146	If it were in my power
	7	248	You may ask if all
	15	230	I make war with what
	27	403	This is my theory
14	7	203	What is happiness?
	10	204	As a person's happiness
	15	413	Happiness is contentment
16	1	268	The cause of man's misery
	5	352	People never seem to have
	12	214	Our opinions are the
	23	320	Happiness is not
	28	149	Every one must answer
17	1	243	If I can show that man's
	10	193	Instead of your
18	9	253	A man may be scientific
	24	266	I wish to make you
19	1	144	The two worlds may be
	19	310	How do I know I have
	26	374	To teach Science is to
	30	203	By establishing the
20	1	397	By the gospel of Truth
	12	264	In mathematics
	20	294	Astronomy has destroyed

Healing Wisdom		Source	Healing Wisdom
Page	Line	Page	Quotation begins
20	27	365	Now it is not to be
21	1	259	Science, like an
	12	329	All Science is
	16	243	Now Jesus cured
	31	328	Every science has
22	1	240	Science cannot
	3	294	Error is wilderness
	8	240	The world of opinions
	14	183	Ideas come forth
	25	168	All Science is a part
	27	242	If Science rules
	30	286	Science is Wisdom
24	9	288	The two characters
	14	135	Awake from your
	26	165	As God is Wisdom
	28	257	Our beliefs, thoughts
25	4	276	Wisdom is the true man
	7	288	Here is the conflict
	8	401	How many persons are
	11	190	No man should have
	13	400	The man who is rich
	16	184	Wisdom contains no
	20	285	The Wisdom that acts
	26	327	Opinions are like a
	32	418	This world is the
27	9	225	The Wisdom of God
	14	327	To give the truth
	25	307	To know that God
	26	367	To know God is to
28	1	167	God is truth and
	3	409	He is all Wisdom
	8	330	Now where is God
	13	324	God is a Spirit
	16	C 253	My God speaks
	24	323	God is not a man
	26	408	My God is Wisdom
	30	323	God is the name of
29	1	324	Man has invented
	9	323	The Christian's God
	17	329	I will give you
	21	324	The time will come

Healing Wisdom Page	Line	Source Page	Healing Wisdom book Quotation begins:
29	25	167	Man's God is all
	31	276	God or Wisdom has
32	10	179	I found that by
	14	180	Now the word mind
	18	182	Mind is a spiritual
	23	180	The word fire
	24	192	So mind is the name
	28	408	The idea that matter
	29	41	The time has nearly
33	1	72	All persons are to
	also	275	(every person is to...)
	4	202	The body may be
	16	202	The mind is the medium
	27	272	We are all taught
	26	231	Mind to me is not
	28	284	It is this: all opinion
	30	268	Mind, like the earth
34	Case	C 272	also C 12 and C 260
36	9	57	What we believe
	11	49	Beliefs make us act
	15	61	Man is governed by
	19	326	A belief contains no
	25	346	There is a vast difference
	32	280	Make man responsible
37	1	27	Whatever is true to a
	4	167	When you have arrived
	10	210	The magicians and
	23	276	God or Wisdom has
	26	189	I believed as all others
38	1	352	People never seem to
	7	259	If man knew himself
	14	220	To separate us from
	20	193	If you embrace the world
39	Case	C 261	If two persons agree
43	Introduction		Collie page 9
46	9	269	Every disease is the
	15	135	All disease is only
	15	351	Disease is an error
	16	234	Disease is the natural
	20	135	The belief is of man

Healing Wisdom Page	Line	Source Page	Healing Wisdom Quotation begins:
46	23	75	Diseases are like
	26	211	All persons believe
47	1	263	I know that a belief
	4	61	Conventional cures
	9	C 289	I will stop here and
	28	322	You tell me I "look
48	7	264	Take the small-pox
	14	268	According to the world
	19	269	Small-pox is like a
49	1	270	Small-pox is a reality
	5	270	I tell you a lie
50	1	C 329	I have been 20 years
	15	C 340	...falling of the womb
	30	35	Man is made up of
51	5	61	The creating of
	8	C 249	I have said that fear
53	Case	C 249	I once visited a sick
54	10	C 268	The child is an idea
	18	278	Children are not
	24	C 274	There is a language
55	1	C 274	The trouble is the
	6	257	It is an undisputed
	Case	257-258	A woman brought
56	25	196	The wisdom of the
57	17	197	I contend that
	27	279	The child is affected
58	Case	308	To show the effect
60	9	75	There is a principle
	24	191	Doctor Quimby, with
	30	415	When sitting by a
61	5	322	Doctor Quimby never
	11	346	My theory teaches me
	13	194	By my theory or truth
	17	280	I destroy the disease
	20	165	My cures are in my
	23	280	I will state a case.
	30	260	To such I stand in
	34	124	I feel that if you
62	14	C 330	Then there are other

Healing Wisdom Page	Line	Source Page	Healing Wisdom... Quotation begins:
62	31	277	There are a great
63	1	291	I have observed
	5	75	If physicians would
	9	47	The cure is not in
	11	56	All medicines affect
	14	260	All drugs when taken
	17	C 249	When Miller prophesied
	22	192	Dr. Q. comes to the
64	Case	78	I often find patients
65	9	190	Every phenomenon in
	12	321	The greater number
	16	319	The basis of Dr. Quimby's
	33	327	Every man has two
66	1	341	A clairvoyant state
	13	342	To make a good
67	8	247	I will now take a rose
	17	414	The minds of individuals
	20	320	Spiritual matter
	30	C 218	Can Dr. Quimby be in
68	6	C 105	What is a clairvoyant
69	6	257	It is an undisputed fact
	16	322	By thoughts we are all
	20	78	Now when I sit down by
70	Case	78	I was sitting by a lady
72	9	195	What has a man to contend
73	1	394	To fight the life of
	5	265	Science first comes to
	18	266	The medical faculty
74	1	374	The world will oppose
	8	241	The blind guides who
	14	267	The great obstacle in
	22	183	I have said that when
	31	278	The medical faculty
75	1	260	Physicians will admit
	7	278	Religious sects fight
	11	388	So in the church the
	15	414	When I say that I know
	21	415	Is it a sin to know this
	25	259	Aristocracy never complains

| Healing Wisdom | | Source | Healing Wisdom |
Page	Line	Page	Quotation begins:
79	9	204	It is easier to talk
	16	202	I have no religion
	21	184	There is a vast
	26	208	As I have the Bible
	32	203	One of Christ's
80	7	383	Goodness was considered
	14	379	Religion is what it was
	16	295	Religion makes no
	19	384	This was the way with
	21	294	You will see religion
81	1	261	The fact is that
	2	378	Does the priest call
	9	256	As the priesthood was
	18	169	The knowledge of man
	25	380	I do not throw the
	31	304	I will give you the
82	8	230	All my writings are
85	10	209	Jesus taught and his
	17	122	Eighteen hundred years
	23	272	If Jesus should appear
	28	204	All religion that
86	6	409	Christ is that unseen
	12	340	Jesus taught Christ
	13	384	To talk wisdom is
	17	351	If you claim to be a
	19	299	To be a follower of Jesus
	23	346	To be a follower of Christ
	25	237	Jesus was called the Son
	29	C 304	At the time of Jesus
89	9	206	I have no account with
	30	209	All people pray to a
90	7	205	Can any good come out
	28	207	I look upon church-
91	1	351	We are taught to believe
	6	210	The priests would offer
	10	352	Each army prays that God
	13	215	Jesus said "Not all who
	17	211	A prayer made up of words

Healing Wisdom Page	Line	Source Page	Healing Wisdom... Quotation begins:
93	9	407	I use words merely for
	14	336	Every person who was
	18	327	When the senses shall
	25	418	It is a common remark
	31	101	The fact is that the
94	1	370	You see how all those
	10	373	Man has to get up a
	12	370	This upset what Jesus
	18	402	Man is always dying
	25	406	There is no good in
	28	C 261	If you want the satisfaction
95	1	209	The religious people
	3	332	The priests tell their
	9	241	An expedition is fitted
	20	407	Our next world is here
98	10	414	The poor soldier who
	24	324	Jesus saw through all
100	9	187	Love is an element of
	19	343	What is the element
	29	297	You see a person
101	1	411	A child knows its mother
	23	187	The laws of love are
	27	188	Love is a substance
102	10	395	As the soil of California
	17	235	Women have more of the
	23	387	Women have more endurance
	29	395	But a female coming forward
103	1	393	The male creation
	8	394	But man from some cause
	15	395	Now where is woman placed
	20	395	Where is woman's true
	26	393	The spiritual rib that
104	1	190	The identity of woman's
	12	160	—the sonnet—
106	10	167	I know I am writing this
	17	80	Now to remind you of what

Foreword

The Coming of the Greatest Science

Dr. Quimby was not only a philosopher but a brilliant scientist who discovered the true cause and cure of disease after long years of diligent laboratory experiments. And it may be said of him "Rare are the men who can rise to the heights of unbiased calm in their search for truth; even more rare are those who having found truth, dare to proclaim it in its pristine and untarnished form before the world." [1]

Since Dr. Quimby wrote his notes, few if any have been able to heal as he did. This is not because he did not leave us sufficient information on the subject, but because this science "is acknowledged by the wisdom of the five senses. It requires more senses to put man in possession of this science." [2]

So it is not only a matter of learning but a matter of reaching to a certain spiritual development which will allow the healer to heal by discerning the thoughts of others. This spiritual development Dr. Quimby called the Christ or the clairvoyant state of consciousness. Lacking this development, his students will have to resort to questioning their patients to find the errors in their thinking. And he tells us in his teachings what these errors are that cause disease.

Besides other titles, Dr. Quimby calls his science *The Science of Correcting an Error* since it "embraces every part of man's reason and destroys opinions on all subjects which tend to disturb man's happiness."

He teaches that an error cannot be corrected by a belief, only by pure reason, which leads to understanding. "A belief is one thing and wisdom is another." It is true that faith plays an important part in our development, but even faith must be governed by reason and fact."(1)

Dr. Quimby's "Science of Health and Happiness" heralds the coming of the greatest science the world will ever know. It is the coming *Science to Heal the Sick*. It was taught by Jesus two thousand years ago but was never known of until now. At last, it is here to stay, as it could have been prophesied by St. John the Divine in the Book of Revelation. He said: "Behold, I have set before thee an open door, and no man can shut it."

So let us "strive to understand" and to realize that "Science is the voice of God."

Erroll S. Collie

(1) Arvid Reuterdahl, *Scientific Theism*
(2) This and other unmarked quotations are the words of Dr. Quimby.

Doctor Erroll S. Collie transcribed and compiled *The Unpublished Writings of Phineas Parkhurst Quimby*, which is the source of some of the quotations used in this book. Doctor Collie is the author of *Quimby's Science of Happiness; A Non-medical Scientific Explanation of the Cause and Cure of Disease.*

Foreword

The Enduring Significance of P. P. Quimby

Nowhere in literature or history, outside the Gospels, so far as I can discover, is there another personage like Phineas Parkhurst Quimby.

Out of rugged, practical New England which was sending its ships and sailors around the world, producing inventors and thinkers who changed the world, emerged the greatest pragmatist of all. Quimby actually left this ordinary, material world and traveled, adventured and explored the immaterial world of mind and spirit. Like Jesus, he came and went at will and like the scouts of Moses he brought back evidence of the other world and demonstrated the existence of the two in such a way as to be indisputable and confirmatory of all the ancient truths in an intellectually satisfying manner.

There is a whole system of philosophy – more instantly helpful and pleasingly practical than any other I know – in his simple proposition: "Man acts as he is acted upon." All right-minded people recommend the Golden Rule. Quimby, alone in modern times, showed how to put your feet where your mouth is.

There is a whole system of psychology in his discovery: "I found that my thoughts were one thing and my beliefs another...if I really believed a thing, the effect would follow whether I was thinking of it or not."

There is no religion in Quimby if by religion is meant a belief or rite or system of salvation; for where Wisdom is known these are not needed.

Quimby is a Great Original. Like the number *one*, primary and indivisible by any but itself. The books of philosophy, religion, drama, poetry, etc. contain the great truths but they are descriptive only; they give us the verbal picture; Quimby showed the functioning substantive.

It is the dream of several of us that more people will discover the treasure in Quimby's beginnings and go on to develop his Science of Health and Happiness – perhaps a Center for Research and Teaching and Practice.

What moderns will do with his complete works, now being made ready for publication, is not predictable, given the century and a half of neglect and distortion; but I think we have in these works the makings of a revolution in the realm of mind and spirit the like of which has not been since the Carpenter walked in Galilee.

Park, the Clockmaker is also here!

Ervin Seale

Doctor Ervin Seale retired from a long and important ministry in New York City. He wrote the *Introduction* to the 1961 edition of *The Quimby Manuscripts*. Dr. Seale is the leader of the Quimby Memorial Church and Foundation and the author of many inspirational religious books.

In his retirement years, Dr. Seale completed his task of compiling *Phineas Parkhurst Quimby, The Complete Writings*; a three-volume set published and distributed by DeVorss in 1988.

Appreciation

I wish to express my appreciation for the encouragements and comments given by Herman Aaftink, Alan Anderson, Erroll S. Collie, Ervin Seale, and Igor Sikorsky Jr., who have long been students of Park Quimby. Gratitude is due Doctor Collie for his labor In transcribing more than two-hundred thousand words of the unpublished hand-written notes of Doctor Quimby. It is appropriate to acknowledge also the work of Horatio Dresser, the son of two of Doctor Quimby's patients, who edited the first publication of Quimby's notes, in 1921, which is the source of most of the quotations used here. These two compilations have made the present work possible. Appreciation is also due Brent Williams, minister of the Los Altos Church of Religious Science, for his helpful comments, encouragement, and instruction.

Special appreciation is due Doctors Erroll S. Collie and Ervin Seale for the introductory commentaries and for supplying the photographs of Park Quimby. Their determination to keep alive the memory and wisdom of Quimby has made this editor's effort seem worthwhile.

045

7300461R0